THE IMPACT OF REAGAN FEDERALISM ON SOUTH DAKOTA AND SOUTH DAKOTA GOVERNMENT

William O. Farber
Professor Emeritus (Political Science)
The University of South Dakota

Governmental Research Bureau
The University of South Dakota
December, 1984

500 copies printed at a cost of $2.30 per copy.

Introducing a New Series..."*Federal Programs in South Dakota*"

With the publication of this monograph the Governmental Research Bureau is initiating a new series of studies. The *"Federal Programs in South Dakota"* series will focus on the patterns of state and local policy making that are unfolding as a consequence of the New Federalism. It is anticipated that the range of federal block grant and grant-in-aid programs will be analyzed in the coming years. In addition to a concern for how these programs affect state and local policy making, the Bureau will be focusing on how these program changes are impacting individual recipients of services. The Bureau is grateful for the financial assistance provided by the Princeton University Urban and Regional Research Center project supporting the publication of this monograph.

Russell L. Smith
Director, Governmental Research Bureau
The University of South Dakota

FOREWORD

Beginning in 1973, an interdisciplinary group of political scientists and economists began what has now become a ten-year series of field network evaluation studies of the effects of changes of U.S. grant-in-aid policies on state and local governments and the services they provide. Professor William O. Farber was a charter member of the research group that began these studies.

The first study was in sixty-five state and local governments on the effects of the general revenue sharing program initiated under President Nixon in 1972. Twenty-four principal researchers, including Professor Farber, conducted the field research for this study. The research was done at the Brookings Institution; it resulted in two books and a number of articles and related papers, including Congressional testimony, which had an important effect in subsequent Congressional action on revenue-sharing legislation.

The success of this study led to the initiation of further studies of the effects of major changes in federal aid policies. Studies have been conducted by the Brookings group on the effects of the community development block grant, enacted in 1974, and the public service job component of the Comprehensive Employment and Training Act, affectionately know as CETA, now defunct.

A fourth field evaluation study was initiated when President Reagan took office in 1981 to evaluate the effects of his broad-ranging 1981 program of major cuts and changes in federal aid programs for states and localities; this study was based at the Woodrow Wilson School of Public and International Affairs of Princeton University. In all of these studies, conducted on a longitudinal basis, South Dakota and local governments in the state were included in the sample, and the field research was conducted or supervised by Professor Farber.

As part of the Reagan study initiated in 1981, funded by the Ford Foundation, teams of field researchers in fourteen states prepared case-study papers in 1984, which were presented at a conference held at Princeton University in June 1984. This publication by the Governmental Research Bureau of the University of South Dakota is a revision of one of the papers presented at the conference.

The aim of this ten-year program of studies has been two-fold -- to provide useful, timely information for policy makers and to explore new ways in which social scientists, on an interdisciplinary basis, can come to understand the way in which policy changes are transmitted and put into effect in the complex, ever-changing environment of contemporary American federalism.

The most important point I want to make in this Foreword is that the author of the paper presented here has been one of the most active, influential and productive members of this research group over what is now a decade of major collaborative policy studies. Professor Farber is one of the first people we turned to when we began this research, and the choice proved to be just right for us and an important reason why the program of studies described above has kept on track and evolved in the way that it has. Bill Farber knows his subject cold. His dedication, deep knowledge, and abundant good humor have been a source of great personal satisfaction to me and an incalculable asset for these studies. I am pleased to have this opportunity in the Foreword to achieve the twin purposes of introducing this paper on the effects of President Reagan's federal aid policies on the State of South Dakota and indicating the great personal debt all of us who have participated in these studies have to its distinguished author.

Richard P. Nathan
Princeton University

September 4, 1984

PREFACE

"The concept of block grants is beautiful, but the creatures Congress is making under the label *block grants* are ugly mutations of the concept. A hodge-podge of categorical grants coupled to a substantial funding reduction is not a block grant. It is a fraud. Congress's New Federalism is merely the old shell game."

This comment by Governor William J. Janklow, published early in 1982, was to prove unduly pessimistic as applied to South Dakota. Indeed the governor himself, by effecting administrative improvements the new approach made possible, was to demonstrate the advantages of the new flexibility. While Reagan federalism may not have achieved as much as originally anticipated, the new approach was to have some exciting, some desirable, and some unfavorable impacts on South Dakota government. On balance the pluses appear to outweigh the minuses. Federal changes seem clearly to have hastened the shift of the locus of decision-making from the local to the state level, a development already underway. As a consequence, few periods in the state's history have witnessed so much governmental change in so short a time.

This research project on the impact of Reagan federalism on South Dakota and South Dakota government has been undertaken as one of the field network evaluation studies sponsored by Princeton University's Urban and Regional Research Center and directed by Dr. Richard P. Nathan, who has kindly written a Foreword for this publication. As Dr. Nathan points out, the aim of the study has been two-fold--"to provide useful, timely information for policy makers and to explore new ways in which social scientists...can come to understand the way in which policy changes are transmitted and put into effect in the complex, ever-changing environment of contemporary American federalism." As such, this study stresses impacts on *governments* rather than *people.* It should be noted that the frustrations which have attended the preparation of this research study have centered on the lack of reliable data, due in part to changed and lesser reporting requirements, and on the lack of sufficient time. More time is needed to provide perspective. This study embraces only federal fiscal years 1981, 1982, and 1983. A three-year period is too limited a time span to determine trends, especially when observations take place only a year after its conclusion. The danger is that findings are based on insufficient analysis, that more is recorded than is really known.

This study is greatly indebted to the Princeton University Urban and Regional Research Center for providing the research design, indispensable background material, guidance, and helpful criticism. The South Dakota field research has benefited from the invaluable assistance of a large number of persons, most notably Sue Brown (housing), Mike Card (education and labor), Forrest M. Flint (social services), Bill Protexter (intergovernmental relations), Greg Redlin (transportation), and Dan Smeins (legal issues). In preparing and editing the manuscript, Alan Clem and Dennis Graves have been especially helpful. Most important, without Marjorie Bjordal's patience and skill with the mysteries of word processing, this study might still be in preparation.

Finally, grateful acknowledgement is made of the contribution of Dr. Russell L. Smith, Director of the University of South Dakota's Governmental Research Bureau, whose assistance has made this publication possible. The responsibility for the text, however, must remain entirely with the author.

Vermillion, South Dakota   William O. Farber
December 1, 1984   Professor Emeritus
                (Political Science)

CONTENTS

Foreword, by Richard P. Nathan............................. i
Preface iii
Purpose and Research Methodology........................... 1

I. THE SETTING FOR THE REAGAN FEDERAL AID CHANGES
  A. The State of the State: A Profile........................3
  B. Priority Problems in Perspective........................4
  C. The Political Environment.............................5
      1. State Government (General).......................5
      2. The State Legislature..............................6
      3. The Executive Branch.............................7
      4. Local Government.................................8
  D. Fiscal Trends and Present Financial Status...............10
      1. Tax Revenues and Fund Balances....................10
      2. Tax Limitation Movement.........................12
      3. Local and School District Finance...................13
  E. Federal Aid and State Dependance.....................13

II. AN OVERVIEW OF CHANGES IN FEDERAL AID DURING THE REAGAN YEARS
  A. Initial Reaction and Response.........................15
  B. 1982 -- The Year of Major Changes....................17
  C. 1983 --Adjustment and Recuperation....................20
  D. 1984 and Beyond -- Unanswered Questions...............21

III. THE STATE/LOCAL RESPONSE AND THE EFFECTS OF THE GRANT CHANGES: THE SPECIFICS
First Section: A Survey of Fiscal, Programmatic and Regulatory Aspects
  A. Entitlement Grant Programs..........................22
      1. Aid to Families with Dependent Children..............22
      2. Medicaid.......................................24
      3. Food Stamps....................................26

    4. Child Nutrition..26
B. Block Grant Financial Histories......................27
    1. Preventive Health....................................27
    2. Maternal and Child Health Care.................28
    3. Primary Health Care...............................29
    4. Alcohol, Drugs, and Mental Health.............30
    5. Social Services.......................................30
    6. Community Development.........................31
    7. Community Services...............................32
    8. Low Income Energy Assistance..................33
    9. Education Consolidation and Improvement....34
C. Capital Grant Programs..............................35
    1. Federal Highway Program........................35
    2. Mass Transit..36
    3. Airport Aid...37
    4. Energy Conservation..............................37
    5. Wastewater Treatment............................37
    6. Housing...38
    7. Economic Development...........................39
D. Other Programs.......................................40
    1. Urban Indian Health..............................40
    2. Cultural Arts and Preservation..................40
    3. Older Americans...................................40
    4. Legal Services......................................41
    5. Refugee Assistance................................42
    6. General Revenue Sharing.........................42

Second Section: Special Developments and Analyses

E. The 1983 Initiatives..................................43
    1. The Job Training Partnership Block Grant.....43
    2. The Emergency Jobs Bill.........................45
F. South Dakota in the Courts.........................47
    1. Community Services Block Grant................47
    2. Low Income Energy Assistance Program.......48
    3. Aid to Families with Dependent Children......48
    4. Litigation v. Legislation..........................49
G. Institutional and Political Changes.................49
H. Efficiency and Management.........................51
I. Strategy and Mix.....................................52
J. Intergovernmental Relations and State Centralization......53
K. The Changing Roles of Local Governments,
    Planning Districts, and Volunteerism................56

IV. CONCLUSIONS

A. What Really Happened? Testing Hypotheses.............58
   1. "Economy and Efficiency"........................58
   2. Behavioral Responses and Hypotheses...............60
B. The Trend: Will It Bend?...........................62

REFERENCES 63

APPENDIX: Program Funding Changes....................65

PURPOSE AND RESEARCH METHODOLOGY

Few developments in our governmental system are as important as those affecting the distribution of powers and responsibilities between the national government and the states. President Reagan has argued for reducing the federal government's involvement and augmenting the role of the states as opposed to that of localities. The president has argued also that federal welfare programs fostered dependency on the federal government and should be reduced. The Omnibus Budget Reconciliation Act of 1981 (OBRA) embodied the Reagan approach. An extremely significant conclusion of the current Princeton University network studies is that the administration's domestic spending acts, although important in some areas, have been overrated, while the reform of the federal system, enhancing the role of the states, now appears likely to have "a substantial and lasting impact" (Nathan and Doolittle, 1983:97).

The summary, overall findings of the Princeton University report are amply supported by the South Dakota experience as recorded in this publication. The implications of recent developments are only now being understood and appreciated. State government in Pierre, and local government as found in the county courthouses and city halls, have changed considerably during the past decade; the permanance of the change is still a matter for conjecture.

This study focuses on what has actually happened in the 1981-1983 period. The research findings are presented in four parts. Part I sets forth the South Dakota social, economic, political, governmental, and fiscal situation -- the setting in which developments occurred. Part II presents the historical impact of the Reagan program and the state's chronological response. Part III analyzes in detail the state's adjustment to specific program changes. Part IV attempts to explain why the state reacted as it did to funding changes and evaluates programs.

The essential features of Reagan federalism used as guidelines have

1

been: (1) tightening eligibility requirements for entitlement programs to reduce costs; (2) combining fifty-seven categorical grants into nine block grants, which broadened program goals to permit wider state discretion in expenditure of funds and reduced reporting and other requirements; and (3) reducing the extent of federal funding -- in 1982 approximately 13.4% for block grant programs. This study is then basically an account of how these features affected South Dakota government and programs.

The significance of recent developments can best be appreciated by an awareness of state government dependence on federal largess. It might very well have been predicted that South Dakota, with approximately a third of its governmental costs provided by the federal government, would be especially vulnerable to program cuts. The research methodology of this study has emphasized fiscal impacts and the strategy employed by the state in responding to these impacts. As examples: to what extent has South Dakota seen fit to replace cuts and to what extent have service levels been maintained through management innovation?

Other relevant considerations have been changes in policy goals and impacts on governmental organization and administrative procedures. To what extent have "targets" changed? Has the Reagan approach abetted state centralization? Is the legislature losing out in the executive-legislative battle? Have administrative requirements been reduced? As a field network study, the emphasis is on these and numerous other *impact* issues and on the *effects* of policy changes. What this study does *not* do is to explore in depth such changes in recipient characteristics as ethnicity, sex, marital status, and income as well as recipient well-being. These program consequences are beyond the scope of the present inquiry.

I. THE SETTING FOR THE REAGAN
FEDERAL AID CHANGES

A. The State of the State: A Profile

In 1919 South Dakota apparently ranked first among the then forty-eight states in per capita income and in the value per acre of farm real estate. Aside from this fleeting moment of fiscal glory, the state has regularly been listed among the lowest in such matters as population and economic growth, teachers' salaries, and expenditures for social services. It has not been quite "fiftieth in everything" as alleged banteringly by Minnesota Governor Rudy Perpich in his verbal fight with South Dakota Governor Bill Janklow over their respective state's attractiveness to business. But the conception prevails that South Dakota is a second Siberia embellished by a Mount Rushmore, and this image problem persists to the despair of local chambers of commerce (Merwin, 1983: 85).

How does the state rank relatively? Among the more significant 1980 standings and per capita income data as reported by the U.S. Bureau of the Census are the following:

(1) The state ranked forty-fifth in population. In contrast to the national average of 26.26% rural, South Dakota had 53.58% rural population. Only two states had a higher proportion.
(2) The state was forty-sixth in population density -- 9.1 persons per square mile compared to the U.S. average of 65.4.
(3) The state ranked fifth in percentage of persons 65 and over -- 13.18% (tying with Missouri). The national average was 11.26%.
(4) With respect to median household income, only Arkansas and Mississippi ranked lower in 1980. South Dakota's $13,156 compares with a national average of $16,850.
(5) South Dakota was eighth (tying with Tennessee) in percentage of families below the poverty level -- 13.05% compared with 9.58% for the United States as a whole. Of the Indian population, 45% was listed as living in poverty.

3

(6) Per capita income was low and unstable. From 1973 to 1982 it varied from $4,937 to $9,666. During that period of time it increased 85.6% while nationally the increase was 121.7%. South Dakota's per capita income in 1983 was approximately 87% of the national average.

The South Dakota profile thus reveals a relatively poor, rural, sparsely populated state with a high proportion of elderly people. Net out-migration from 1970 to 1980 was 26,384. Nevertheless, the state population as a whole rose 3.7% to attain a total of 690,768 persons --still below the state's high point of 692,849 reached in 1930. The state's neighbors to the east and south -- Minnesota, Iowa, and Nebraska -- have been more prosperous with better balances of industry and agriculture, and to the west and north, North Dakota, Montana, and Wyoming have been lucky in the search for energy resources. South Dakota has remained in the middle, a sort of "hole" for a wealthy doughnut of states.

B. Priority Problems in Perspective

South Dakota's adverse economic status is the rather obvious overriding state problem. The lack of industry and commercial development, the slow population growth, the low per capita income, the paucity of natural resources, the heavy dependence on agriculture, the uncertainties and severity of the weather, and the increasing conservatism of the population (attributable in part to the growing proportion of the elderly and the out-migration of youth), all abet the relative decline of the state's support of services. As the state attempts to confront the adverse factors which affect it, the most obvious challenge is the inability of the state on its own to bring about substantial change.

What happens to agriculture is far more significant than what happens to federal aid programs. As a farm state, South Dakota is important nationally. In 1983 the state ranked first in the production of oats and rye; second in flaxseed and sunflower seed; fourth in spring wheat, hay, and alfalfa hay; fourth in number of sheep and lambs; and fifth in beef cows and durum wheat production. "Price" is king in the South Dakota economy. This situation has an important bearing on evaluating changes in federal funding. Federal funding changes, significant though they may be, are of lesser consequence than the changes in the prices of corn, wheat, and cattle.

Current political issues commanding public attention are not critical or urgent in the sense that doom impends if not immediately or suitably decided. The economic development proposals usually con-

4

sidered have centered on (1) promoting irrigation and construction of water systems, (2) attracting industry through industrial revenue bonds and soliciting business ventures by advertising and direct contacts, and (3) assisting housing projects. Interest rates have been regarded as the principal handicap for both agricultural and industrial expansion. Energy cost problems, aggravated by the severe 1983-84 winter, have also been of concern. Unemployment, with the state rate among the lowest of the fifty states (5.3% compared to the national 8.0% in December 1983), is not regarded as a serious problem. Housing receives attention not because the housing need is critical, but as a way of assisting the construction industry.

In the area of economic development, the state has had, however, some recent spectacular successes. Under the governor's leadership, the state's attempt to attract big banks has received nationwide attention. As *U.S. News and World Report* noted, "The hottest cities in banking these days are not New York, Chicago, and Los Angeles - but Big Stone City, Rapid City, and Sioux Falls, all in South Dakota" (1984:68). Recovery in the state apparently lags behind the national trend, however, and is very uneven geographically (Bureau of Business Research, 1983: 2).

A frustrating problem that seems to defy solution is the relation of state and local governments to Indian tribal governments and the Indian people. At present Indians constitute 6.5% of the state population (44,948) but over half the population in five counties. Unemployment remains officially about 50% (usually estimated to be considerably more) and per capita income remains very low. While the poverty rate in South Dakota was 13.2% in 1980, on Indian reservations it was much higher -- Pine Ridge 43% and Rosebud 40%.

C. The Political Environment

(1) State Government (General). South Dakota's governmental structure remained relatively unchanged on the state level from 1889 when statehood was achieved until 1972. The state had continued to operate under its original constitution and while by 1970 there had been 150 amendments proposed and seventy-five adopted, the changes were of a patchwork type.

The creation of the Constitutional Revision Commission in 1969 resulted in proposals for changing every article of the constitution. Twelve revisions were submitted by the legislature and five were adopted. Four, adopted in 1972, were of great importance: the executive article, which greatly enhanced gubernatorial power, especially in relation to administrative reorganization; the judicial article, providing a unified court system; the local government article, containing self-executing home rule provisions for county and city government; and a new amending article authorizing the constitutional initiative.

The "1972 revolution" came during one of the few times when the state had a Democratic governor. Indeed, with the exception of two years (1959-61), subsequent to 1937 there were only Republican governors until 1971. Since 1979, when the Republicans regained the governorship, there has been only one significant change in governmental structure and that, adopted in 1982, required a legislature based on single-member senate districts.

(2) The State Legislature. The legislative branch has similarly been dominated by Republicans and during 1983 and 1984, the Senate consisted of twenty-eight Republicans and seven Democrats, while the House consisted of fifty-four Republicans and sixteen Democrats. Sessions are now restricted to forty days in odd-numbered years and thirty-five days in even-numbered years. The legislature has been streamlined by the establishment of thirteen parallel committees, including one joint committee (appropriations). Procedures have been modernized. Work is facilitated by study committees functioning between sessions of the legislature, but the two-year terms of all members is thought to restrict legislative effectiveness.

The modernization of the South Dakota legislative branch began in 1951 with the establishment of the Legislative Research Council. Patterned after the Oklahoma council, all members of the legislature belong to the council and have committee assignments between legislative sessions. The result has been an increasingly knowledgeable legislature.

As legislators became more competent, they asserted controls over the rule-making process, but more importantly over the budget. South Dakota has had an executive budget since 1925, and the executive budget has traditionally been the basis of state financial planning. Now called the Bureau of Finance and Management, the budget agency has approximately twenty-four employees. The governor's control over administration and finance was also greatly increased as a result of the adoption of a consitutional amendment in 1972 which required executive reorganization. As a consequence, administration is organized uniformly in fifteen departments completely under the governor's control.

These developments resulted in a corresponding legislative development. The legislature strengthened its capacity to scrutinize the executive budget by making the Appropriations Committee a joint committee of house and senate members, employing a finance analyst, establishing a joint interim committee with power to authorize expenditures in excess of the appropriation law, and appropriating federal aid as well as state funds. Thus no federal aid can be received or spent without express legislative authorization.

The legislature's principal tool in restricting federal aid has been the General Appropriation Act which, as noted previously, appropriates both federal and state revenues and FTE's as well as monies. To change either requires approval of the Interim Appropriations Committee (ten senators and twelve representatives) and scrutiny is not routine. Approval requires the concurrence of a majority of the entire committee membership (twelve votes) so that absences count as disapproval.

(3) The Executive Branch. Despite the legislative developments, the balance of power has recently shifted in the executive direction. The 1972 constitutional changes enhanced gubernatorial control of the executive branch. The terms of the governor and other elected constitutional officers were increased to four years and the governor and lieutenant governor were elected as a team. The veto power, which now included the power of executive amendment as well as the line item veto, further strengthened the executive. With comprehensive budgetary and appointing powers and the power to restructure state government by executive order (subject to a legislative veto), the governor has been well equipped to provide leadership in both policy and administrative matters. Executive power has been further reinforced by the political complexion of the legislature. With over two-thirds of each house Republican, the governor, also a Republican, has encountered minimal political difficulties.

Armed with the new tools, it has not been difficult for the governor to be the key figure in federal aid decisions. If a federal grant became available between sessions of the legislature, the procedure would ordinarily consist of study by the appropriate department and the Bureau of Finance and Management with a final decision by the governor. Then the recommendation would be presented to the Interim Appropriations Committee, which has the authority to accept, modify, or reject the proposal. The significant thing is, of course, that the executive agencies provide the initial input.

What makes the present governor such a potent political force lies only partly in the availability of the necessary constitutional tools. Even more significant has been the dynamic character of Governor Janklow. Now in his second four-year term (he was reelected in 1982 by a 70% majority), the governor arranged for the sale of Missouri River water to a consortium headed by Texas Eastern Corporation;

although the project to ship coal by slurry from Western coal fields ultimately was abandoned, the state netted around $3 million for its treasury. He prevailed upon the legislature in a twenty-four hour period to pass legislation abolishing interest rate restrictions and thus inducing banks to locate in the state, with the result that Citibank now occupies a $25 million complex in Sioux Falls. He arranged for the purchase of 936 miles of Milwaukee Railroad trackage at a cost of $24 million and secured Burlington Northern as the line's operator.

The governor's role in policy matters has been comprehensive and dominating. He has organized an effective group of young assistants -- knowledgeable, energetic, and loyal. Outside his own office, the staffs in the Bureaus of Finance and Management and Intergovernmental Relations have been especially important. There is no doubt who has been in charge in South Dakota. The governor views the major problem facing the state as one of economic development. Thus priorities include an emphasis on telling "the South Dakota story" and trying to induce industry to locate in the state.

South Dakota has been designated the "State of Reluctant Change" (Pierce and Hagstrom, 1983:560). The continued refusal of the state legislature to consider the enactment of corporate or personal income taxes has been made possible by limiting appropriations. The cautious political attitude is often attributed to a disastrous experience in the twenties with rural credits; it resulted in an onerous debt that served as a limiting factor on state government for thirty years.

(4) Local Government. The basic structure of South Dakota's local governments has changed but little in the almost hundred years since statehood. The U.S. Census of Governments reveals that only in the case of school districts has there been much reorganization (See Table A).

Table A

SOUTH DAKOTA GOVERNMENTAL UNITS

	1967	1972	1977	1982
Counties	64	64	64	66
Municipalities	306	308	311	312
Townships	1,050	1,034	1,009	996
School Districts	1,984	228	198	196
Special Districts	106	136	147	199
TOTAL	3,510	1,770	1,729	1,769

In 1967 South Dakota had the dubious distinction of being the most governed state in the United States; there were fewer persons per unit of government in South Dakota than in any other state -- 192 persons per unit. Since 1967, thanks to school district reorganization, South Dakota's unique position has been lost. Nevertheless, the number of small units remains excessive. In 1982-83, for example, eighty-nine of the 184 public school districts (48%) had enrollments of less than one hundred.

When the state constitution became effective in 1889, state leaders envisioned a rapidly growing state. Population had more than doubled between 1880 and 1890, reaching 348,600. The governmental structure established then contained numerous units of local government as well as public institutions; it was designed for a population of several million and contemplated cities of over 100,000.

The result of this overly optimistic planning was too many counties, too many small towns, and too many schools with resultant inefficiencies. In 1980, twenty-four of the state's sixty-four counties had a population of less than 5,000 but were operating under the same form of government found in Minnehaha County with 109,435 persons.

In the face of this situation, the need for larger units to take over governmental functions and the need for cooperative arrangements become greater. Fragmented tax resources and taxing units with greatly varying tax capacity make the case for centralization that much stronger. But in the four major functional areas of local government -- education, welfare, transportation, and corrections -- changes have been slow. Thus the question of how federal involvement has affected these relationships is an important one.

Two developments in the past ten years have been especially significant in state-local relationships. Beginning in 1974, state aid to education increased rapidly. In that year it rose from $15,119,835 to $21,119,835. Thereafter it was to increase dramatically until in 1984 total state aid to education was $55,388,403, an increase per student of over 400% from 1974.

The other centralizing development was the phasing out of the personal property tax beginning in 1979. As part of this action, the state agreed to provide replacement funds which now total approximately $41 million. Since the amount fixed for reimbursement has remained essentially unchanged since 1979, local governments have been the loser in this shift of revenue sources and to a degree, the loss of the personal property tax revenues has reduced the effectiveness of the increases in state aid.

How federal funding and funding cuts have impacted state-local government and intergovernmental relationships will be the subject of later comment. Federal funding has tended to preserve the status quo. Whatever the cause, South Dakota has been slow to change government structurally. County government remains much as it was established in 1889. No counties and only two municipalities have the manager form. Almost 1000 township governments still exist and receive general revenue funds, although functions are limited mainly to highway maintenance, snow removal, weed control, and the conduct of elections. School districts have been reorganized, as noted previously, and in the ten years following 1967 were reduced from 1,984 to 198. Roughly 300 municipalities are governed in accordance with forms and procedures legislatively and precisely prescribed, and although home rule has been an available option since 1972, no municipality and only two Indian reservation counties have taken advantage of it. The two outstanding characteristics of South Dakota local governments are their small population base and the absence of professional staff.

D. Fiscal Trends and Present Financial Status

If a South Dakota governmental ten commandments existed, the first and greatest would be one requiring a balanced budget. The one lesson all South Dakotans seem to have learned is the principle of fiscal conservatism. Uncertainties, of income produce a caution reinforced by early tragic experiences. The state constitution, as a consequence of the state's economic fluctuations, continues to contain limitations on taxes and indebtedness. A balanced state budget is required under the penalty of imposing a state property tax of up to two mills if needed, and this trigger mechanism has been sufficient to ensure that no budget remains unbalanced.

(1) Tax Revenues and Fund Balances. The net result of the state's fiscal conservatism has been an excessive reliance on the sales tax at the state level and on the property tax at the local level. There is no general income tax, either personal or corporate, and this has been a source of state pride among conservatives.

The sales tax has had the advantage of reflecting steady and inflationary growth. The statistics for the past five years and for total general fund receipts are shown in Table B.

Table B
STATE GOVERNMENT REVENUES
(in thousands)

	Sales Tax	General Fund	Federal	Total Operating	G.F. Balance
FY 1979	$130,821	$172,658	$153,740	$473,570	$ 10,869
FY 1979	140,656	142,174	229,530	512,629	16,467
Fy 1980	140,656	142,174	229,530	521,629	16,467
FY 1981	144,936	149,684	258,032	591,495	20,458
FY 1982	159,809	165,113	251,315	584,440	19,716
FY 1983	164,154	169,479	268,343	627,804	18,599

Note: Sales tax receipts are included in General Fund. Data are taken from *State of South Dakota Governor's Budget* for appropriate years.

There are only two special earmarked dedicated funds of consequence in the state -- the Highway Fund (gas tax and licenses) and Game and Fish Fund (licenses). The data for these funds as found in the governor's budgets are as follows (see Table C):

Table C
DEDICATED FUNDS

Highway Fund (in thousands)

	Total	Federal	Ending Cash Balance
1979	$113,923	$46,843	$37,756
1980	132,717	61,625	25,245
1981	133,537	55,697	13,624
1982	133,017	56,861	21,134
1983	138,487	56,799	33,117

Game and Fish Fund (in thousands)

	Total	Federal	Unobligated Balance
1979	$ 4,581	$ 1,089	$ 1,759
1980	5,549	1,638	1,966
1981	7,226	1,706	2,153
1982	8,486	2,329	2,661
1983	9,551	2,502	3,792

The revenue trends for county, municipal, and school district governments are shown in Table D:

Table D
LOCAL TAX LEVIES

	County	City	School District	Total
Tax Levies (in thousands)				
1979	16,017	33,648	74,756	124,458
1980	16,643	34,313	75,648	126,604
1981	16,550	36,802	83,802	137,226
1982	17,025	37,082	84,313	138,420
1983	18,186	37,560	85,141	139,432

(Note: Special district levies are included in the total.)

The above data underscore the stable and gradual growth character of the state's principal taxing jurisdictions.

Significantly, however, tax increases have not kept pace with inflation. While the CPI changed 32.01% from 1979 to 1983, total property tax levies increased only 12.03%. Some cities have, however, resorted to sales tax levies. The situation is graphically illustrated in the Advisory Commission on Intergovernmental Relations publication, *1981 Tax Capacity of the Fifty States* (GPO, 1983 p. 61). If South Dakota had a "representative" tax structure, in 1981 the state and local governments would have taken in $43,217,000 more in revenue. While the state has somewhat improved its tax effort, no personal income tax has been imposed and only a very limited corporate tax.

(2) Tax Limitation Movement. Despite the relatively low tax burden, South Dakota has not been immune to tax limitation agitation and in the seventies a movement primarily based in the western part of the state developed considerable strength. Partly in response to the movement, the legislature in 1977 proposed a constitutional amendment which prohibited an increase in the tax rate on income or sales or the valuation of property unless adopted by popular vote or by two-thirds of the members of each branch of the legislature. Thus any change in the sales tax rate, the principal source of general state revenue, would face a formidable hurdle.

The proposed amendment, endorsed by the Republican party and condemned by the Democrats, was approved by the voters in November, 1978, by a vote of 116,647 to 103,621 (53.0%). It became a part of the state constitution as Article XI, Sec 13. A "Dakota Proposition" modeled after California's famed Proposition 13 was overwhelmingly defeated in 1980 (Carlson, 1980).

(3) Local and School District Finance. Many smaller jurisdictions (municipalities and school districts), declining in population and suffering financial trouble, will not be able to assume greater responsibilities if federal aid and state services decrease substantially. Local governments have, however, received help in the past six years with (1) the abolition of the personal property tax with full reimbursement to local governments by the state, and (2) regular, substantial increases in state aid to education, which mitigated the need for local property tax increases. Nevertheless, the most obvious source of added local government revenue -- an increase in the property tax -- seems to be generally unpalatable in the light of present conventional wisdom that says property taxes are too high. As evidence of this, property tax for low income property owners has been frozen.

The situation with respect to counties has been different from municipalities. By means of frugal spending habits, counties have conserved their assets to the point of arousing considerable criticism. Many counties had sizable "savings" accounts. The consequence was state legislation in 1981 (SDCL 1981, Ch.56) which provided: "The total unobligated balance of all funds may not exceed forty percent of the total amount of all appropriations contained in the budget for the next fiscal year." One of the possible effects of decreased federal funds may be placing greater responsibilities on county governments. Perhaps this can be done through county-city cooperative arrangements. This is now in the "talking stage" with few specific proposals.

The principal state budget/tax limitation is the one found in Article XI, Section 1. This limitation mandates balancing the state budget by requiring tax levies in any year subsequent to an unbalanced budget. The mechanism implementing this provision has been spelled out in statute (SDCL 10-12-1 to 10-12-4) and since legislators are wary of tax increases, this threat has been sufficient to prevent enactment of unbalanced budgets. Even the possibility of such a situation would almost certainly result in preventive action such as occured in 1980.

E. Federal Aid and State Dependence

South Dakota has always been a winner in terms of federal aid. In

1981, according to a Tax Foundation, Inc. report, the state ranked fourth in receiving aid per tax dollar. In that year the state received $1 for every $.60 paid in federal taxes. The estimates were $212.8 million in taxes compared to $353.8 million in aid (Sioux Falls Argus Leader, 1982: 1A).

As might be anticipated in a conservative state, federal monies have been consistently regarded with suspicion. This skepticism is confirmed in the use of general revenue-sharing funds. On the state level they became part of state aid to education and were regarded as apart from the regular state budget. On the local level counties and municipalities initially refrained from using funds except for one-shot needs or the support of ancillary activities. (See SDCL 4-8A and 8B.)

Federal aid on the local level is especially significant with respect to education. According to statistics provided by the U.S. Office of Education, 9.8% of educational funding in 1979-80 could be attributed to the national government; South Dakota's percentage was 15.4. From state sources nationally the percentage was 46.8 and for South Dakota 23 (1983:42).

II. AN OVERVIEW OF CHANGES IN FEDERAL AID DURING THE REAGAN YEARS

A. Initial Reaction and Response

The Reagan victory in November, 1980, made it clear that a change in national-state relationships was probable. The South Dakota governor's office was able to stay on top of developments primarily because of line department contacts and extensive preparations by the Bureau of Finance and Management. Indeed, after the 1981 legislative session, the Commissioner of the Bureau of Finance and Management initiated meetings on the subject which were attended by budget and planning staffs as well as Legislative Research Council personnel. In addition, staff attended federal briefings by the Denver federal regional office. Throughout the summer, close communication between line departments, the budget office, and the governor was maintained.

An example of the initial interest in and enthusiasm for the Reagan approach is to be found in the submission by the governor of a comprehensive and ambitious *South Dakota Human Services Block Grant Proposal,* subtitled "Give It a Whirl." This proposal, dated March 20, 1981, was submitted directly to the president by the governor. The proposal covered (1) Youth and Family, (2) Elderly, (3) Food and Nutrition, (4) Health, and (5) Energy Assistance. It proposed that the state take over programs in these areas and begin administering them October 1, 1982.

The South Dakota proposal was not accepted, probably in part because federal officials as well as the Congress were in the process of hammering out the essential features of the Reagan approach. The main features of the program were finally revealed in the Omnibus Budget Reconciliation Act of 1981 (Public Law-97-35), signed August 13, 1981, and destined to be called OBRA.

OBRA was a comprehensive act consisting of twenty-seven sections. With the noteworthy exception of defense, almost the entire gamut of national government activities was covered. The act achieved substantial savings primarily by reducing spending authorizations and

15

changing eligibility rules and benefit formulas of entitlement programs (Elwood, 1982:23). The estimated reduction in outlays ranged from $36.9 billion in budget authority to $51.2 billion.

Meanwhile the South Dakota Legislative Research Council created a special Subcommittee on Federal Budget Impact headed by a co-chairman of the Appropriations Committee. This committee met on June 12, 1981, to be briefed on the subject and witness a presentation by a staff member of the National Conference of State Legislatures. Headlines such as "Cuts May Suck Millions from S.D." (*Sioux Falls Argus Leader*, 1981) were enough to compel legislators as well as bureaucrats to scrutinize carefully the potential impacts of probable cuts. A news release of October 1, 1981, the date the new block grants became effective, indicated South Dakota's probable loss for the health and social services block grants alone as $3,350,000.

One of the critical areas causing immediate concern was federal impact aid, that is, payments made in lieu of taxes where there were federal installations. This aid, amounting to about $14 million dollars in South Dakota, was distributed to about fifty school districts. Six school districts received over half their total budgets from impact aid. Sizable cuts were anticipated which could result in school closings. Another potential problem area was highway construction, where a federal cut of $7 million was anticipated for FY 1983.

During the fall of 1981, the line agencies with functional ties to Denver and Washington had tried to follow the reconciliation process and keep the governor informed. It appears that department heads were as knowledgeable as they could be under the circumstances. In November, in anticipation of a $3.8 million cut in Medicaid due on July 1, 1982, the Interim Health and Welfare Committee recommended that the governor consider combining the Departments of Health and Social Services to reduce costs.

After the presentation of the governor's budget on December 8, 1981, and prior to the meeting of the legislature on January 5, 1982, it became increasingly clear that the governor had become the dominant force in determining the state's response to the Reagan approach. This was underscored when it became apparent that no public hearings were to be required for fiscal 1982 and significant public participation and legislative involvement were not to occur. The legislature, when it met in 1982, was confronted with a *fait accompli.*

By the time the legislature met to begin its regular session on January 5, the governor had labeled block grants "a fraud" and predicted "a reduction of a lot of programs." All six block grant programs available for acceptance by October 1, 1981, had been accepted

16

by South Dakota. The acceptance was solely by the governor; there was no consultation with the legislature. It was not strange, therefore, that legislators were disturbed by their lack of input in the acceptance of the block grants.

At the same time, it was clear that the governor was empowered to act and that in terms of budget preparation, prompt acceptance made possible an adjustment to fiscal realities that administrative uncertainties would have precluded.

When the governor presented his 1983 budget to the legislature (December, 1981), the Omnibus Budget Reconciliation Act had been in existence three months and the main features of the Reagan approach were clear. This made possible the submission of a budget predicated on potential cuts, and the governor was able to speculate with respect to varying impacts. At the time, he predicted that the principal areas to be cut would be in the Departments of Labor, Social Services, Health, and Vocational Rehabilitation.

B. 1982--The Year of Major Changes

The cuts, when they came, appeared severe. A comparison of funding changes (see Appendix A) provides ample justification for the initial alarm expressed by the bureaucracy and interest groups. The alarm was to prove premature, for it gradually became apparent that the cutbacks were more of an indication of the future direction of social programs than an actual, immediate reduction in services. There were significant alleviating factors: (a) many social and educational programs carried over appropriations from the previous year which allowed them to absorb the shock of the reductions; (b) in other instances, (e.g., child nutrition), considerable cash balances had accrued in the school districts, allowing them to replace the subsidy reductions; (c) planned expansions and new programs were simply dropped when word of the reduced funding became available (social services block grant), forcing the agency to live within its means but without any reduction in former service levels; (d) management, forced to act, responded by reallocating limited resources to achieve the same goals; and finally, (e) the major contract authority programs in the capital construction area require several years time before the full effects of the reductions can be measured. The group most affected by the cutbacks was the administrative staff who lost their jobs, not the recipients of services.

The most innovative response South Dakota state government made to the changes of the federal level was in the mental health area. In the past, the community mental health centers received foundation grants directly from the federal government; the Office of Mental Health distributed Title XX funds and the community support system grant to the centers; and the state's primary mental institution, the Human Services Center, was independently administered through a third agency, the Board of Charities and Corrections. The fragmentation of the funding sources (federal and state) had created three independent agencies charged with similar missions, but cooperating only superficially with little knowledge of what and how well the services were being performed by the others. With the legislation authorizing the consolidation of the alcohol, drug, and mental health grants, the state had the opportunity to merge all three agencies under a single umbrella agency. This was done by a joint powers agreement signed May 1, 1982, thus providing for comprehensive administration of mental health services under the control of the Human Services Center in Yankton.

On the fiscal side, South Dakota state government had neither the financial resources nor the political will to replace much of the funding in programs reduced by the Reagan administration. The absence of protest groups was attributed by some to the probability that few deserving persons were hurt or that other aid possibilities were available. Those affected may have been scattered, few, and politically inept. Among the state departments immediately affected by the loss of federal funds were the Department of Labor (where employment totalled 340, down almost 200 from 1977), the Department of Education and Cultural Affairs, and the Department of Social Services. Public Service Employment (PSE), which had provided training for as many as 1,373 clients in 1980, was destined to be phased out.

New and significant eligibility restrictions applied to three entitlement programs -- AFDC, Medicaid, and food stamps -- and resulted in a decrease in the number of recipients; but changes in total funding for AFDC, as well as for Medicaid and food stamps, were inconsequential. (See Appendix A.)

The people most affected by the federal reductions and policy changes were AFDC households. (See III-A-1.) A number of cases were closed due to federal program changes. These closed cases were, of course, no longer eligible for Medicaid services. No data have been available as to how many of these closed cases had taken out a private health policy or requested general or medical assistance from the county. Due primarily to the unborn child provisions and the 150% standard of need, there was a decrease in the number of assisted families from 6,559 in September 1981 to 5,675 as of July 30, 1982 -- a drop of 884.

The proposition that people have been more affected by the budget cuts than jurisdictions is probably not as clearly discernable in South Dakota as in most states. The fact that South Dakota did not have a full-blown AFDC program by itself limited the potential numbers of people who might be affected. The lack of a medically needy program also limited the potential affected population. The state chose to continue the existing programs and services with only minor modifications. This resulted in large additional expenditures in the Medicaid program to minimize the reduction of federal reimbursement as well as an increased utilization rate at a time when the state had limited financial reserves.

In the case of food stamps, the provision limiting the eligibility of households of 130% of the poverty line did not have a significant effect due to South Dakota's low per capita income. Of the affected groups, the changes in eligibility seem to have impacted college students the most. As will be noted from Appendix A, the total federal funding for AFDC, Medicaid, and food stamps increased in 1982. Child nutrition, an entitlement program, was cut, and this is one of the few South Dakota examples of where there was replacement. (See III-A-4 below.)

Of the block grant programs, the largest funding cut was in the social services area, where the cut was estimated at $2,692,965 or 20%. The exact impacts are described in III-B-5 along with the state's reaction. What was done appears to be a remarkable job of innovative financing. A significant change occurred in the administration of the community development block grant where priorities were notably shifted. (See III-B-6 below.)

A substantial loser was the community services area, where the immediate effect was to cut off funding for three of the six community action agencies which blanketed the state. The manner in which this was done caused a protest which became the basis for a lengthy legal controversy. (See III-B-7 and III-F below.) Job Service and CETA programs were cut almost as severely and the PSE program came to an abrupt end. (See III-K.) The substantial CETA carry-over cushioned the shock of this cut.

It is difficult to assess the health block grant impacts because of the way the programs were administered prior to 1982. The nature of the impacts is presented in some detail in III-B.

Most of the capital grant programs received substantial cuts in 1982 --highways, airport aid, energy conservation, wastewater treatment, and new Section 8 housing. The impact in these areas was substantially minimized by the nature of the construction industry. That is, contracts made in 1981 were being implemented in 1982, so there was a significant carry-over effect. For specific reactions to each of these program funding changes, see III-C below.

C. 1983--Adjustment and Recuperation

The year 1982 had been one of great uncertainty. Such headlines in the South Dakota press as: "Indians Preparing for Cuts," "Cuts May Cut Millions from S.D.," "Reaganomics Starting to Strike," "Federal Aid Bill Could Close Some S.D. Schools," and "Federal Aid Bill Cuts to Curtail Highway Construction" had put all South Dakotans on the alert to the possibility of disaster.

As 1983 started to unfold, it became increasingly clear that the second round of cuts was not to occur and most agencies had sufficient carry-over monies to minimize fiscal impacts. When the governor submitted his budget in the 1983 legislature, he was able to recommend a balanced budget with no new taxes and a 4% cost of living adjustment for state employees. His budget message was replete with references to cuts--some serious, some trivial. Thus the Tie-Line operation, which gave citizens free telephone access to state agencies and was funded by the community services block grant, would hence forth be supported at a lower level, and callers would be charged $1 per call. There would be a personnel reduction in the energy conservation program. But the Department of Social Services received an augmentation of state funding of almost $3 million to take care of increased Medicaid costs for fiscal '84 and $1 million for the fiscal '83 shortfall. On the other hand, the health services, also hard hit in 1982, recovered only slightly in 1983. Nevertheless, by improved management, fund shifting, and carry-overs, impacts were to prove minimal as will be described at length in Part III of this report. The CETA reduction, over $4 million in 1982, benefited in 1983 from a $1.3 million carry-over.

The mental health program, reorganized in 1982, received unusual gubernatorial and legislative support. In anticipation of federal cuts, the 1982 legislature appropriated an extra $300,000 for the program and in 1983, $1.2 million was added -- a singularly large replacement of a federal funding cut. By contrast, the alcohol and drug abuse programs, also cut, received no augmentation. The three community action programs not supported in 1982 under the drastically cut community services block grant continued to be unfunded.

In two areas recovery of funds was to begin in 1983 --

20

transportation and energy conservation. In the case of transportation, federal funding was to be up almost 50% over 1981. Energy conservation, after receiving over a $1 million cut in 1982, had recovered substantially in 1983 and was destined to be fully recovered by 1983.

What substantially changed the 1983 picture was, of course, the federal jobs bill, which was approved by the president March 24, 1983. The Bureau of Intergovernmental Relations was given the task of monitoring the numerous "shots in the arm" and by July 7, 1983, the bureau was able to report that expenditures were, for the most part, on schedule. See III-E for a full account of the allocations.

An examination of the programs analyzed in this study reveals 1983 as a year when the realization grew that the cutting process had slowed down and indeed, turnabouts were in evidence. For the most part South Dakota governments, both state and local, were apprehensive of the 'morrow, but not to the degree of a year earlier.

D. 1984 and Beyond: Unanswered Questions

When federal fiscal year 1983 drew to a close on September 30, South Dakota state officials were preparing the 1985 state budget. The governor in his December 1983 budget message recommended increased funding for state aid to education and funding for water development. The proposed 1985 budget was, of course, a balanced one. It reflected the governor's priorities, which were to be generally accepted by the state legislature. The Department of Water and Natural Resources received a $5 million dollar increase. The governor noted that because of increased federal funding, highway construction contracts would be up $21 million.

But the state retained its cautionary attitude toward federal funding. In 1983 the legislature created an inflation stabilization reserve fund into which any ending cash balance over $5 million was to be deposited. At the end of FY 1985 the fund should have a balance of $3.4 million -- the reserve for a proverbial rainy day. The cloud which hung over South Dakota's future was not so much fiscal insecurity as the quality of its services.

III. THE STATE/LOCAL RESPONSE AND THE EFFECTS OF THE GRANT CHANGES: THE SPECIFICS

Part II of this report presented an overview of the historical developments which took place in federal aid during the first three years of the Reagan administration. In this part, the impacts on specific programs will be presented along with a discussion of special problems affecting South Dakota. The three principal types of federal grants are: entitlement, operating, and capital. As will be apparent later, impacts have varied by grant type.

First Section: A Survey of Fiscal, Programmatic and Regulatory Aspects

A. Entitlement Grant Programs

Entitlement grant programs have the most direct impact on people. As explained in *The Consequences of Cuts* (Nathan, Doolittle, and Associates, 1983:14):

> "Entitlement grants are made to states and localities, which in turn make transfer payments to families and individuals. These payments can be in cash or in kind, such as those for medical care, food stamps, and school lunches.
>
> Typically, state and local governments are reimbused by the federal government for some portion of the entitlement payments they provide to eligible persons. A key characteristic of these programs is that all persons eligible for aid must receive it; state and local governments cannot regulate caseloads by appropriation actions."

The three largest entitlement programs are aid to families with dependent children (AFDC), Medicaid, and food stamps.

(1) Aid to Families with Dependent Children. While the attempts to reduce entitlement program costs centered about changing eligibility requirements, there were other changes as well. In the case of the

AFDC program, the more significant were listed in the Princeton study (1983:26, 28) as follows:

1. Allowed states to require certain recipients to work in public agencies and for private firms in exchange for welfare payments.
2. Decreased the amount of earnings and other income that is disregarded in calculating how much assistance a recipient should receive. (Formerly the first $30 in earned income plus one-third of the amount over that had been excluded in the calculation of benefits.)
3. Imposed an absolute income ceiling on eligibility, so that no one earning more than 150% of the state standard of need could receive aid.
4. Ended payments to strikers, students over eighteen, and women pregnant with first child until the sixth month of pregnancy.
5. Required that a portion of a stepparent's income be treated as available for support of an AFDC stepchild.
6. Required states to use a retrospective accounting method, under which a grant is based on the recipient's actual income in the previous month rather than the expected income in the coming month. Recipients must report their income each month.

It should also be noted that each state was permitted to calculate its own standard of need, which might be below the federal poverty line. This South Dakota as well as forty-six other states did in 1982, resulting in lower benefit payments.

While there are no reliable statistics showing the extent to which eligibility was lost in South Dakota because of the new requirements, some examples can be given. In 1982, 258 individuals were denied benefits because income exceeded determined need; in 1983 denials totaled 265. In counting income, South Dakota considered food stamps and rent or housing subsidies. There was a failed attempt to require the inclusion of Indian trust land in the declaration of resources (see III-F). If successful, more than 300 Indian families would have been denied payments. The state estimated that a total savings of $1,435,000 for itself and $3,055,000 for the federal government was attributable to the new income requirements.

Another important rule was the one limiting eligibility to children under the age of eighteen who are completing high school. According to a report from Minnehaha County, caseloads dropped by 12% for fiscal 1982; earnings and gross income limitations were the more significant causes of caseload decline. The regulation relative to strikers has little importance in South Dakota.

A special comment needs to be made relative to WIN-CWEP (Work Incentive-Community Work Experience Program). This program, actually authorized by 1967 amendments to the Social Security Act, has proved popular in South Dakota, and in 1981 the legislature specifically authorized the Department of Social Services to develop a plan for the implementation of workfare (SDCL 28-1-54 through 58). OBRA was the enabling federal legislation that permitted the state to establish a Community Work Experience Program (CWEP) and this was done by the Department of Social Services through a contract with the Department of Labor in April, 1982. The major goal has remained: to assist AFDC applicants and recipients in entering unsubsidized employment. Economic self-support and independence, and therefore welfare savings, would result. AFDC recipients are required to participate in CWEP as a condition of eligibility for AFDC. Exemptions included those over sixty, those actively involved in a full-time approved program or already employed at least eighty hours a month, or those caring for a child under age six.

Since April 1982, over 100,000 hours of public service work has been performed by CWEP participants statewide. At the end of November, 1983, there were 1,957 AFDC recipients enrolled in WIN. Job Service works with all of these clients. The data from the seventeen reporting points (April 1, 1982, to December 31, 1983) do not present convincing evidence of the extent to which clients were dropped for work refusal. Of the recipients, about 25% were de-registered for one reason or another but obviously there were many reasons for case closings. The Department of Social Services feels that the real worth of the program is in the extent to which placement in productive work has occurred in a high percentage of cases.

In any event, the costs of AFDC did increase from $17,252,522 in 1981 to $17,389,519 in 1982, and $20,513,181 in 1983. The federal contribution declined in 1982 but by less than $100,000.

(2) Medicaid. This program is the largest single social service program in South Dakota and, as noted previously (see II-B and C), there were no "savings" during the three years covered by this study. Indeed, Medicaid costs rose from $75,011,539 in 1981 to $81,521,013 in 1983 and are estimated to exceed $100,000,000 in 1985. The state, chiefly from general fund dollars, picks up approximately one-third of the cost. There has been no legislative resistance to the program. In fiscal

1983 there was a small amount of malt liquor tax used as part of the state contribution (less than $200,000), and beginning in fiscal 1984 the counties have been asked to contribute a total of $611,000 in return for the payment of some county medical obligation.

In FY 1982 the state received a $966,682 cut. The normal two-to-one South Dakota match was reduced 3% in 1982 and this amount was made up in the state's 1982 appropriation. In its 1982 plan for maintenance of essential social services in light of reduced federal funding, Medicaid services were supplemented in part with excess general funds from other departments, including funds transferred from the low income energy assistance block grant.

For state FY 1983, employment-related day-care for AFDC caretakers was shifted from Title XX payments to vendors to an employment-related expense calculated into the Title IV-A grant to the recipient. This, in effect, has made the recipient more responsible for arranging day care services as well as absorbing some of the cost of day-care when compared to the old vendor payment system.

Federal changes to the Medicaid program had little effect on providers and recipients in South Dakota. The state had a relatively bare bones Medicaid program (for example, no medically needy program) for categorically eligible recipients. The reduction in the federal reimbursement rate resulted only in a shifting of costs from the federal government to the state -- no benefits were impacted as a result of this action.

The following changes occurred in the state's Medicaid program:

1. Transfer of assets provisions were strengthened. This had only a minor effect upon the Medicaid nursing home budget due to the very small number of cases involved.
2. The state received a Title XIX waiver for services to the developmentally disabled. This allowed South Dakota to accelerate its deinstitutionalization process and provided much more flexibility in providing services to the developmentally disabled in the least restrictive environment. It has also, in effect, resulted in cost-shifting from local school districts to the federal Medicaid program.
3. Unrelated to the federal changes, the state implemented a policy whereby the nonfederal matching funds for Title XIX services to handicapped children are provided by the school districts. This includes services provided at the Crippled Children's Hospital and School and Title XIX services to the developmentally disabled in a non-institutional setting.

South Dakota did not eliminate any of its optional Medicaid services. In short, what the state did for AFDC and Medicaid was to replace any federal cuts so that for 1982 there was no total decrease and by 1983 there were substantial increases.

(3) Food Stamps. The OBRA sought to lower food stamp costs, as in the case of AFDC, by restricting eligibility for those with other incomes and by imposing new administrative requirements. (The key changes are listed in Nathan et al, *The Consequences of Cuts,* p. 33.) Probably the most significant way that eligibility was reduced, however, was the change in AFDC recipients. Such recipients were automatically eligible for food stamps.

The 1982 food stamp funding cut produced no state reaction. The program was regarded as a federal program and responsibility for the cuts was that of the federal government. There were, however, additional demands on non-profit charitable organizations and a state division of volunteerism was established. Furthermore, there were stepped up activities in the distribution of state commodities. The Office of Volunteerism, created in 1982, was able to distribute surplus commodities with a minimum of cost. The number of distribution points was increased six-fold to well over 300.

The federal food stamp cost as reported by the Department of Social Services was $2,364,901 (administration) plus $24,501,443 in coupons in 1983, compared to $1,848,261 and $20,369,350 for 1981.

(4) Child Nutrition. This program was severely impacted in 1982, with a cut in funding from $11,740,767 to $9,215,082. This resulted in a drop in reimbursement from $.15 to $.10 per meal. To make up for the loss in funding, school districts have subsidized meals with district general funds or raised the cost of meals or both. In some cases, districts reviewed food service staff scheduling, purchasing, and portion allotments. In at least one instance a management review was undertaken.

Beginning in 1982 the U.S. Department of Agriculture required filings as a basis for determining free meals, and starting in 1983 at least 3% of the filings must be verified. Participation in the program declined but how much can be attributed to changed requirements and how much to declining enrollments is difficult to determine. Federal funding in 1983 increased to $11,200,179 and in 1984 will be approximately $12,000,000. The state's required contribution has been: 1981, $758,651; 1982, $734,981; and 1983, $750,000. Meals are now compensated where they are free at $1.0875, up 10% from 1983.

B. Block Grant Financial Histories

State and local reaction to the OBRA initiated block grants varied considerably by grant. As the following summaries rather dramatically show, it is no easy task to portray what are complex and sometimes inadequately reported developments. To what extent did the attempt to give the states greater control over funding result in improved delivery of services? Did funding cuts cause service deterioration? To what extent did the state replace cuts? Which services benefited from carry-over funds? These are among the questions considered in this section of the report.

It should be noted that operating grants include more than the principal block grants discussed in this section. Other operating grants are analyzed in III-D below. Operating grants are of two main types, as noted in the Princeton study (1983:15): *"formula* grants allocated to states or local governments on an automatic basis, as specified in statutory law or administrative regulations, and *project* grants, for which a federal agency considers individual applications for particular activities and projects."

(1) Preventive Health. In 1981, the Budget Reconciliation Act initiated the preventive services block grant. The three categorical grants South Dakota had been receiving in this area, hypertension control, risk reduction and health education, and comprehensive public health services, were consolidated into the new block grant provisions. The total consolidated amount of funding was approximately $50,000 less than the state had been receiving under the categorical grants.

The state's response was not to replace the lost revenues, but to set priorities within the areas of allowable use of the preventive health block funds. This resulted in curtailing plans to develop a statewide hypertension screening program, including the reduction of one state staff position and associated administrative costs. This effort had not previously been considered a state health priority, but when federal funding became available, the effort was initiated. The new law required continuation of hypertension activities at 75% of the old categorical amount in FFY 1982 and phased it down over four years, at which time the mandatory minimum requirement will be discontinued. To do this, the state is annually reducing funding for hypertension services by its community health nurses.

In the areas of risk reduction and health education, the state's response was also not to replace the lost funds, but to reduce the old categorical effort which was not yet fully established. The contract with the South Dakota Lung Association expired and was not renewed. The administrative staff and support expenses were also reduced. Because the effort was tied to a broad purpose of promoting good health habits, it was considered a mission that other health activities would absorb. Public health services activities of the state utilizing 314(d) funding were not reduced. These services were viewed as deserving the highest priority in the use of the block funds.

The change to the preventive health services block grant program thus has had little impact on South Dakota. The funding cut has been sustained by discontinuing the further development of relatively new projects just getting underway. Federal funds continue to be used in the general categorical areas and have not been shifted to other allowable block grant areas (these are basically the areas of other categorical grants that were consolidated into the block). The cuts have been in aspects of projects that the state considered low priority. The state had previously been starting hypertension and risk reduction efforts more in a response to the availability of funds than out of a sense of need for these services. State or the other replacement funds have not been sought because the projects cut were not considered of a high enough priority to warrant new replacement resources.

(2) Maternal and Child Health Care. This block grant combined existing programs for maternal and child health, crippled children, certain disabled children, sudden infant death syndrome counseling, genetic testing, lead-paint poisoning prevention, hemophilia treatment centers, and adolescent pregnancy grants. Prior to its enactment, South Dakota had categorical grants in four of the eight areas identified in the new statute: maternal and child health, crippled children, disabled children's program, and sudden infant death syndrome. The total consolidated amount of funding was approximately $200,000 less than the state had been receiving under the categorical grants.

As with the preventive health block grant, the state's response was not to replace the lost revenues, but to set priorities within the allowable areas of fund usage with the MCH block grant provisions. Although carry-over funds were available at the time, there was a recognition that on a continuing basis the funding cut would be felt. Therefore, program changes were made to adjust to the new funding level and priorities. In this adjustment to the $200,000 cut, South Dakota responded much in the same manner as other states by eliminating most of the program project activities and specialty staffing. Overall, the regulations and restrictions of the program were vastly decreased in both program and administrative areas.

One change that this MCH block grant did bring was matching requirements of 57% federal and 43% general. However, for South Dakota this did not require any new state funds because general funds in the crippled children's program were already present that could be used as match.

Shortly after MCH program changes were implemented in order to adjust to the $200,000 cut, the jobs bill was passed and brought an additional $470,000 into the MCH area. This has meant that the state now had more money in this area than it did under the old categorical grants, and far less federal requirements.

In summary, according to program officials, the change to the MCH block grant has had a favorable impact on South Dakota. Federal funding cuts have been replaced and increased by the jobs bill; program changes have been made to eliminate what the state considered low priority and ineffective projects. Funds are now used to fund MCH projects that the state considers to be of greatest priority. Also, carryover provisions now give the state two years to plan and spend the funds, thus increasing the state's flexibility to meet changing needs.

(3) Primary Health Care. This block grant finances community health centers (CHC) and rural health initiatives (RHI) in the states. In the past, federal statutes and regulations provided only for federal management by the regional offices of these activities in the states of a region. The change to the primary care block grant made an option available to the states to take over the administration of these federal projects underway in the states.

Prior to its enactment, there were approximately 30 CHC or RHI federal projects in South Dakota. These projects provide health care in areas designated as medically underserved areas. These areas and assigned staff were being supervised directly by the Denver regional office. The largest project in the state was the community health center in Sioux Falls, which was allocated approximately $300,000 a year.

South Dakota did not take advantage of the opportunity to take over the management of these activities. If an application is not submitted, the language of the block grant provides that these activities be retained under the management of the federal government. Several reasons have been given for non-participation. First, there is a 25% state match for the first year, and because this is not a current state outlay, it would mean the need for new state dollars. Second, CHC's were often regarded with suspicion by the private medical community.

They generally involve the designation of a "medically underserved area." Furthermore, the primary health care block grant lifted no restrictions or regulations from states, since they were not involved with administering those projects prior to enactment.

(4) Alcohol, Drugs, and Mental Health. This block grant combined existing programs for community mental health centers; mental health systems; comprehensive alcoholism prevention, treatment, and rehabilitation; and drug abuse prevention, treatment, and rehabilitation.

Prior to its enactment, South Dakota had been receiving categorical grants for all of the programs identified in the new statute. However, funding for community mental health centers did not pass through state government before this block grant program began, so the amount of actual reduction in funding is difficult to determine.

With respect to mental health, administration was substantially changed in 1982 with the transfer of major responsibility from the Board of Charities and Corrections to the Human Services Center (Yankton). Consistently, the program was rapidly becoming decentralized and deinstitutionalized with the development of eleven community health centers. (See II-E.) The program has had strong gubernatorial and legislative support as shown by the $1,200,000 replacement of federal funding in 1983. (See Appedix A-6.)

In 1983 the alcohol, drug abuse, and mental health block grant was $3,140,000. Five percent of the total became "governor's discretionary money." Of this amount, 33.8% was given to the alcohol and drug abuse program and the remaining 66.2% to mental health. To this the governor added his discretionary money; the bulk of the funding goes to the mental health centers. Carry-over funds along with some reductions in the alcohol and drug areas and increases in the mental health area have avoided any significant cuts from occurring to date. However, it is recognized that unless replacement revenues are generated, particularly in the community mental health centers, cuts will become necessary in the coming years. Initially the program was assisted by the "forward funding" of the new block grant; that is, money was available from the federal government at the start of the fiscal year rather than on a reimbursable basis.

(5) Social Services. This block grant continued the funding of programs previously supported by Title XX of the Social Security Act. The state's total funding cut was 20%, a substantial loss. Among the programs involved were child day-care, counseling, protective services for children and adults, and homemaker services. The state's response to this loss in revenue can best be described as "creative financing and

public management.'' South Dakota undertook initiatives to maintain essential services in light of this major funding cut. It chose to address the situation by: 1) *cutting* low-priority social service activities, 2) *shifting* some social service costs to other federal funding sources; and 3) *supplementing* the social services block grant with federal funds transferred from the low income energy assistance block grant.

A total of $494,000 in social services activity cuts were distributed as follows: training and staff development-related activities, $99,000; emotionally disturbed children program, $67,000; day-care, $67,000; professional and clerical salary and operating expense, $199,000; computer services, $32,000; and Tie-Line $28,000,

Approximately $400,000 in social services costs were shifted from social services block grant funding to other federal fund sources, including: $47,000 in mental health administrative costs to the alcohol, drug, and mental health block grant; $300,000 in homemaker costs to Older Americans Act (Title III-B, funding previously earmarked for Community Action Programs outreach activities); and $53,000 in foster care costs to child welfare service (Title IV-B, funding previously earmarked for the emotionally disturbed children program). These changes -- along with shifting approximately $703,000 in day-care costs to the AFDC grants program (Title IV-A) and approximately $915,000 in mental health services costs to Medicaid (Title XIX) and the alcohol, drug, and mental health block grant -- accomplished the task of meeting the funding reduction.

In addition to the cuts and shifts just described, approximately $975,000, or 10% of the low income energy assistance block grant was transferred to the social services block grant. Given the flexibility to implement these initiatives, the reduction in federal funds for social services was addressed with little impact on essential social services in the state, in the opinion of program officials.

In summary, the change to the social services block created the largest funding cuts to South Dakota. By discontinuing plans for new services that had not yet begun, eliminating some low-priority items, and refinancing other essential services, some potentially serious impacts were minimized.

(6) Community Development. The community development block grant is distinctive in that here the state had an opportunity to utilize its own rather than national priorities in the distribution of funds. In an unequivocal way, the priority was determined to be water projects. Thus in 1982 numerous water systems, flood control projects, storm sewer installations, sewer line replacements and the like were subsidized. This emphasis has continued in fiscal years 1983 and 1984. The

grants are made with the stated purpose of promoting more rational land use, expanding low and moderate income housing, increasing economic opportunities for low and moderate income persons, and correcting deficiencies in public facilities affecting public health, safety, or welfare.

Available federal funding increased from $6,111,000 in 1981 to $7,856,000 in 1983. The 1983 funding included $1.1 million from the Jobs Bill. Fifty-two awards were made in 1982 and forty-six in 1983. There is no state money in this program and on the state level it is administered by two FTE's. The program is a popular one and has been completely under the control of the governor's office.

The governor has maintained a strong interest in this program, and his emphasis on water projects has been questioned by legislators. In FFY 1983 the state was required to match 10% of the total allocation in community development dollars with "hard" or "soft" dollars, but this requirement has been waived for FFY 1984 and future years. In FFY 1983, the state was required to match, on a dollar for dollar basis, the amount of administration claimed from the allocation. In FFY 1984 and future years, the state may use the first $100,000 of "administration" with no match required, and then match on a dollar for dollar basis any amount required over that up to a maximum of 2% of the total allocation. Less than $70,000 annually has been used for administration. Project proposals are carefully evaluated on a point basis. The grant program is administrated by the Department of Water and Natural Resources.

(7) Community Services. This block grant program has been the most controversial in South Dakota. Prior to 1982, the six community action agencies which blanketed the state received funding rather evenly distributed on what was in effect a pass-through system. When under OBRA the state received discretion through the block grant approach, the governor made the decision not to fund three of the CAP organizations, a decision which was protested in the courts. (See III-A.)

The community services block grant produced an available $1,011,944 in 1982, a sharp decline from 1981's $1,820,736. By 1983 funding was reduced to $803,109 and in 1984 to $971,074. The South Dakota grant application for 1985 asserts, "In the true spirit of the block grant, the state will be able to concentrate on specific or general projects as the need arises and exercise ultimate discretion in funding decisions to 'get the best bang for the buck.'"

The principal use of funds has been to assist community action agencies; three of the state's six agencies have continued to receive substantial support. In FFY 1981 the six CAP's had received a total of $931,748 and Indian tribal governments $218,000, but in 1983 this was down to $227,840 for the CAP's alone. In addition, Tie-Line ($33,000), the Volunteer Office ($80,000), and the Association of Senior Citizens ($15,000) received funding. The decision as to which agencies are supported has been solely that of the governor, and this has been the subject of both legal and political controversy.

On the political side, in 1984 the South Eastern Human Development Agency (Sioux Falls) did not receive funding nor did the Greater Missouri CAP. The Minnehaha legislators (Sioux Falls) were somewhat concerned with this action, but it was west river legislators who introduced a bill (SB 169) in the 1984 legislative session requiring that "the federal funds received by the state from the community service block grant shall be used to provide opportunities for community service activities statewide." The legislature took no action on this bill, but the governor's request for an authorization to spend $734,041 in 1985 was increased in the General Appropriations Bill (SB 220) to $884,041 so that additional federal funds could be expended for community action agencies. This action is significant because it is almost a unique example of an attempt by the state legislature to involve itself in block grant administration. The large 1984 carry-over is necessitated by the pending law suit.

When this block grant was accepted by the state, the governor designated the State Planning Bureau (now Bureau of Intergovernmental Relations) to administer the program. The head of the bureau (Commissioner of Intergovernmental Relations) reports directly to the governor.

(8) Low Income Energy Assistance. This program received a dramatic increase in funding in 1983 -- $11,010,851 compared with $5,184,560 in 1981 and $5,821,637 in 1982. Because of climatic conditions, this program receives continuous attention in South Dakota. Eligibility for energy assistance payments has depended on whether recipients received AFDC supplemental security income payments, food stamps, or payments under the Veterans' and Survivors' Pension Improvement Act of 1978. Households with incomes not exceeding the greater of 150% of the state's poverty level or an amount equal to 60% of the state median income are also eligible. Despite the demands for assistance, carry-over in 1983 was $2,623,609. In 1983 grants totaled $7,073,569, weatherization programs $1,918,936, and transferred to social services was $1,279,290. This program contains no state money, and since there have been no cuts, there has also been no need to make replacements.

(9) Education Consolidation and Improvement. To understand changes in fiscal support for this block grant, funding for Chapter I and Chapter II should be considered separately. The respective funding levels in South Dakota for the first three Reagan years have been as follows:

	1981	1982	1983
Chapter I	9,979,814	8,855,210	8,960,516
Chapter II	2,000,000	2,000,000	2,187,360

Chapter I of the Elementary and Secondary Education Act of 1965 is the principal basis of federal aid to the nation's elementary and secondary schools, providing financial assistance for compensatory instruction to educationally disadvantaged children in low income areas. The program includes no state monies; only federal dollars are used. The distribution formula is weighted so that districts with low income and disadvantaged students received proportionately more aid. The funding has increased slightly and for 1985 will be up 5%. The program is "forward funded" so that schools can plan ahead.

The Chapter II funds are divided 80% to local educational agencies (LEA's) and 20% to the administering state department. Schools receive funds based on special project applications for a wide variety of programs including career education, metric education, law-related education, and ethnic heritage programs.

Fiscal impacts appear to be minimal in the change from the categorical grants to the ECIA. There is no real gain or loss in services or funding. The formula for allocating the funding is different. The entitlement is based 90% on enrollment, 5% on special education enrollment, and 5% on the sparsity of the population.

The brunt of the cuts have been borne by the state education agency. Three full-time equivalents were lost in the original shift, and more cuts are expected. An effort is being made to shift three FTE's to general funds.

The ECIA, a consolidation of twenty-nine categorical grants, operates not as a block grant but rather as a pass-through grant. The state agency no longer considers applications on a competitive basis; the local education agencies are "entitled" to funds based on the formula. The school districts must permit local participation and allow for local discretion by involving "parents, teachers and others" in the planning. The state staff reviews applications merely to determine that the IFA's intended use meets the intent of the law. The entitlement system is popular with school districts which may use the aid for projects they would be hesitant to support with local funds.

The way the new approach is implemented is illustrated by the Sioux Falls experience. Most of the twenty-nine folded-in programs did not apply to Sioux Falls; many, for example, applied to school districts with integration problems. The block grant provided for distribution of the funds on the basis of school-age population. Since South Dakota received the total available for all programs (even though previous funds had not been fully utilized), Sioux Falls and the rest of the state substantially benefited by the new approach. Thus, under Title IV-B of the Elementary and Secondary Education Act, Sioux Falls previously received $45,000 for library resources and science equipment. Now, under the block grant, $200,000 is available and the permissible uses expanded so that such items as staff development and innovative administrative functions are legitimate objects of expenditure.

C. Capital Grant Programs

Capital grants differ from entitlement and operating programs in that there is ordinarily a long interval between the time funds are appropriated and when they are actually spent. This means that the impact of cuts will under any circumstance be delayed and there are greater opportunities to cushion shocks by innovative actions. The most sizeable federal grants for capital purposes are for highways, housing, and wastewater treatment, all important to South Dakota.

(1) Federal Highway Program. Of all the programs benefiting from a quick turnabout, the highway program was the most fortunate. Not only has federal funding increased, $56,135,622 in 1981 to $76,949,347 in 1983, but the state has been able to provide needed matching dollars. While there have been no important programmatic changes affecting the transportation department, there has been a new emphàsis on management and efficiency measures.

The nearly 50% increase in federal funds from FFY82 to FFY83 was a result of the passage of the Surface Transportation Assistance Act of 1982 (STAA). The increase in state funded match in FFY83 ($4,822,000), was met with unobligated reserves in the State's Highway Trust Fund. These reserves had accumulated after an excise penny on motor fuel tax had been levied in 1981 for railroad purposes but had been found unconstitutional. The tax was left on, however, and deposited in the highway fund. In FFY 1983, $1,745,000 dollars included in the Emergency Jobs Bill of 1983 for South Dakota was allocated for South Dakota highway purposes.

While the figures show a substantial increase in funding for highway construction, South Dakota's percentage share of the total funds available has actually been declining. Formula changes in the Interstate 4R program, implemented under the Federal-Aid Highway Act of 1981, resulted in the state receiving approximately $6 million less in FFY 1983 than it would have under the old formula. In the primary program, formula changes in the STAA of 1982 resulted in South Dakota receiving approximately $1.7 million less than otherwise would have been the case.

There have been no substantive program changes in DOT programs as a result of the increase in funding authorized under the auspices of existing programs. The State Department of Transportation has not changed the percentage split it uses to divide two categories of funding, secondary and bridge replacement, with the counties.

While the need to reorganize the field maintenance operations administratively had long been recognized within the department, action was not taken until June 27, 1983. The principal motive for the reorganization was not contemplated as an effort to raise the additional matching funds required over the life of the STAA of 1982 (approximately $25 million), but it did have the effect of generating sufficient savings for the next four years to preclude the department from requesting any increase in its current tax base to match the additional federal funds. The reorganization closed fourteen maintenance shops, three subdistrict headquarters, and one district office. Ninety-eight positions were abolished as a result of these closings. Estimated state fiscal year 1984 savings are $1.9 million, and $3.9 million annual in state fiscal year 1985 and subsequent years.

One significant regulatory problem should be noted. Section 105(F) of the STAA of 1982 required that states contract 10% of their highway construction funds with disadvantaged business enterprises (DBE). This new requirement has presented a difficult challenge to the state (South Dakota's minority population is approximately 8%) in light of the fact that in FFY 1982 our DBE participation was 0.2%. In FFY 1983 the percentage increased to 8.2, and FFY 1984 year-to-date percentage (February 20) is 11.03%. One additional staff person was transferred into the civil rights program, which now has a greater emphasis on certification and compliance activities in this area.

(2) Mass Transit. South Dakota received federal funds under sections 16(b) (2) and 18 of the Urban Mass Transit Act. From the former, federal support for 1981, 1982, and 1983 has remained at $189,000 with a small state supplement; for the latter, federal funds decreased from $507,491 in 1981 to $439,177 in 1983. The level of the latter

funding is considered by South Dakota transportation officials to be sufficient for all current needs of existing public transportation systems. The demand for (16) (b) (2) money is considerably in excess of available funding. Approximately 65% of the funds are awarded on the basis of grant applications to provide vehicles for the elderly, the remainder for those developmentally disabled.

(3) Airport Aid. Airport aid suffered a significant cut in 1982, declining from $2,311,952 to $1,824,259. In 1983 it increased to $1,972,021 plus $116,667 from the Emergency Jobs Bill. The South Dakota Department of Transportation provides technical assistance in the design, application, and construction supervision process of the Airport Improvement Program (AIP). The airport owner -- most airports are owned by cities in South Dakota -- is the ultimate winner or loser in funding changes. The reduction in federal funding from 1981 to 1983 ($339,931) has been offset by the cities' ability to receive discretionary funding available under the AIP. South Dakota officials estimate that cities each year have qualified for discretionary funds equal to approximately twice as much as is available for primary airports. The bottom line is that the funding for airport construction during 1981-1983 has increased at or close to levels that meet South Dakota's airport capital structure replacement needs.

(4) Energy Conservation. A capital grant program which did suffer in 1982 was the Energy Conservation Program, which in 1981 received $3,202,681 and in 1982 $1,932,495. While in 1981, 2,162 homes had been weatherized, in 1982 the number was down to 1,473. Since a majority of those assisted were elderly and handicapped, this was a serious reduction. But in 1983 available funds had been increased to $2,490,034 with 2,477 weatherized homes and in 1984 the estimated funding was $4,056,496.

(5) Wastewater Treatment. Federal wastewater treatment grants have been administered in South Dakota by the Office of Water Quality in the Department of Water and Natural Resources. From a high point of $22.4 million obligated in 1978 and 1979, funding dropped to $11.8 million in 1982. In 1983 and 1984, $11.9 million was available, $1.6 million of which included carry-over funds in 1984. There has been no replacement with state funds.

Since this program began in 1977 projects in fifty-three communities have been completed and thirteen are under construction. Match has been on a 75% federal, 25% local basis, but effective October 1, 1984, the federal contribution will be reduced to 55%. A total of $120 million worth of projects remain unfunded so that while substantial progress has been made, as replacement needs arise the demands for a high level of funding will continue.

In 1982 the EPA required a revision of grant criteria to better reflect the need for water quality improvement. The state department maintains a priority list for future funding and grants are made with the approval of the regional EPA office in Denver. This program is highly regarded by local communities. Sioux Falls received $2.2 million in 1983, plus $1.1 million previously awarded; Aberdeen received $2 million. The 1984 funds have only recently been received and will be awarded and made available early in 1984.

(6) Housing. South Dakota housing programs are administered by the South Dakota Housing Development Authority. The authority's principal programs are (1) HUD Section 8, New and Substantial Rehabilitation; (2) HUD Section 8, Moderate Rehabilitation; (3) HUD Section 8, Existing; and two state programs, (4) Mortgage Subsidy Bonds -- Home Ownership, and (5) Mortgage Subsidy Bonds -- Rental Housing. There has been a significant South Dakota reaction in this area as the size of the tax-exempt revenue bond issues indicates.

The most important change in federal housing policy as it affects South Dakota has been the loss of the Section 8 "new" program last available on a statewide basis in 1981. Some moderation of impact occurred because of the length of time necessary to bring new or rehab units to occupancy (up to a year or more), the existence of a large inventory of "new" units from previous commitments, and an occasional direct allocation of Section 8 units to special projects (a Sioux Falls vocational-rehab school received a forty-eight unit allocation for a $1,600,000 project with an annual contract authority of $239,000 in 1983).

The continuation of the state's home ownership program, which has assisted hundreds of moderate and middle income families each year, and modest increases in the "existing" program have also helped blunt the problems caused by loss of Section 8 "new." On the other hand, the impact of this loss was magnified by a recession-induced reduction in unsubsidized housing production, and a temporary cessation in the delivery of additional "mod rehab" units to South Dakota (an unfortunate coincidence) at the same time.

Because of the slow rate of new unsubsidized construction and the slower rate of expansion in Section 8 availability, rental vacancy rates across the state dropped (to around 1% throughout 1983 in Sioux Falls) and rents rose with demand. Working and other poor -- already paying a higher percentage of income toward their assisted rent under Reagan policy -- more often had difficulty finding units with acceptable rents. At the same time, waiting lists of families needing assistance in Sioux Falls and other areas of the state grew to record levels.

In an effort to stimulate construction, help some of those in need, and stabilize rents, the State Housing Authority initiated a rental housing bonding program in 1983. Twenty percent of the 314 units financed will be made available to low and moderate income families. The program accounted for nearly 20% of the units started in Sioux Falls in 1983. After a smaller FY 1984 issue, the state legislature, which favored individual home units, attempted unsuccessfully to halt apartment construction financing by resolution.

The state's home ownership program is based on using tax-exempt bonds; but since federal policy (according to the authority's annual report) "essentially prohibits states from using tax-exempt revenue bonds to finance moderate income home ownership for families who had owned a home during the previous three years," the authority feels its ability to provide needed housing is greatly handicapped. The restrictions cut in half the pool of eligible borrowers. This plus high interest rates "are doing an effective job of limiting SD HDA's ability to provide home ownership opportunities for moderate income families." Nevertheless, from November 1, 1974, to October 15, 1984, a total of $1,045,152,235 worth of bonds had been issued.

It will be noted that the Authority seems to stress the plight of the moderate income group. The failure to use the tax-exempt bond revenue for rentals for low income families was the subject of debate in the 1984 session of the state legislature.

(7) Economic Development. Since 1980, Economic Development Administration (EDA) activity in South Dakota has been on a low level. Prior to the Reagan administration, development project grants had totaled between one and one and a half million annually. Now grants are almost entirely of a planning character; the most frequent recipients during 1981, 1982, and 1983 have been the six planning districts, Indian tribal governments, and South Dakota state government. In 1983 there were no public works allocations, only four in 1982, and three in 1981. Such funding apparently is subject to national as well as regional federal approval.

The EDA program is now the most important single source of support for the six planning districts (over $50,000 each). The districts have been the backbone of rural planning in South Dakota. Other funding sources, HUD 701 and Section III of the Rural Development Act, are no longer available. EDA funding has remained constant, continuous, and to the planning districts, indispensable.

D. Other Programs

(1) Urban Indian Health. South Dakota Urban Indian Health, Inc., Pierre, provides medical and dental services to qualified off-reservation Indians by contract with the Indian Health Service. Funding is under Title V of the Indian Health Improvement Act. Funding to this non-profit organization in 1981 was $170,350; in 1982, $132,636; in 1983, $154,126; and in 1984, $165,576. The 1983 and 1984 amounts include funds for a community health representative. (See Appendix).

The 1982 cut necessitated closing the Aberdeen and Vermillion clinics; the Pierre and Sioux Falls facilities have remained in operation. Demands for service have increased with "encounters" listed as 8,600 in 1982, 13,000 in 1983, and over 20,000 estimated for 1984. Volunteers are used and recently doctors have been willing to assist with contributory service. The $11,000 funding increase in 1984 will permit the reopening on a part-time basis of the Vermillion clinic.

(2) Cultural Arts and Preservation. (a) South Dakota Arts Council. The Arts Council in 1981 received $275,000 from the National Endowment for the Arts. This was cut to $250,350 in 1982, but all of this cut was replaced by a state legislative appropriation of $25,000 ($10,000 for the Artist in the Schools Program and $15,000 for local challenge grants). Interestingly, when in 1983 the National Endowment restored its cut with a $282,700 allocation, the legislature increased its appropriation to $45,000. In 1984 the legislative grant was $55,000 while the federal funding was $285,600. (b) The South Dakota Committee on the Humanities received $324,000 in federal funding in 1981, 1982, and 1983, but suffered a reduction of 7% in 1984 ($302,000). In all four years the committee also received $75,000 which could be used as challenge match for local programs.

(3) Older Americans. In 1980 a total of 23,335 South Dakota families were considered to be living in poverty. The 112,739 persons were about one in every six persons, or 16% of the state population. Of this number 10,426 were sixty-five years of age or over. While this was a decline from 19% to 11% of all elderly families, recent projections by the South Dakota Department of Labor estimate poverty totals to include 18,800 elderly persons by 1984, or 19% of all elderly persons (Satterlee, 1983).

The special programs dealing with senior citizen poverty have been those under Title V of the Older Americans Act, which funded the Green Thumb Program administered since 1965 by the Farmers Union, and much smaller programs of AARP (in Minnehaha County not eligible for Green Thumb) and the Forestry Department. A new initiative is the TAP program (Training and Placement) for older citizens. Funds for fiscal 1984 total $105,000 of which 15% ($15,750) is allocated to administration. Thus far less than fifteen elderly are in the program. Eligibility is much stricter than for Green Thumb and compensation must be matched, whereas Green Thumb is 100% financed.

Green Thumb funds were $1,300,000 for FY81 and FY82 ($1,381,000 for the two-year period July 1, 1981-June 30, 1983). The attempt to cut funds in 1982 (4%) was thwarted when Congress overrode a presidential veto. Fiscal year funding for 1983 and 1984 has remained at approximately the same level. Present recipients (March 19, 1984) number 422. It should be noted that the governor in this period added $691,000 from his Title V discretionary fund and $438,000 during the current year. In addition, the American Association of Retired Persons (AARP) in Sioux Falls (administering the same program for Minnehaha County only) is supervising forty-five recipients with a total recipient budget of $147,000. There is also a small -- less than fifteen recipients -- allocation for forestry projects.

(4) Legal Services. South Dakota is blanketed by three legal service agencies receiving funding from the Legal Services Corporation: East River Legal Services (Sioux Falls), Black Hills Legal Services (Rapid City), and Dakota Plains (Mission). The budgets of all three were subjected to a 25% cut in 1982. A development in the East River and Dakota Plains office since 1983 is the "Judicare" approach, a system of private bar involvement. This may eventually supplant the employment of full-time lawyers. The system has caused East River Legal Services to close offices and employ attorneys on a contract basis, thus permitting clients to use attorneys closer at hand. Service in some cases may actually have improved. As a result of the 1982 cuts, Black Hills Legal Services closed its Hot Springs and Spearfish offices.

Of the three offices, Black Hills Legal Services has been most successful in securing additional funds. From the R.G. Smith program of Howard University, $20,896 was secured in 1981, $27,667 in 1982, $16,800 in 1983, and $11,200 in 1984. The Legal Service corporation allocations since 1981 are as follows:

	1981	1982	1983	1984
East River	570,639	422,238	422,238	458,931
Black Hills	212,226	160,613	160,613	172,158
Dakota Plains (Basic)	176,363	141,153	141,153	163,404
(Native American)	625,639	588,622	588,622	671,677

(5) Refugee Assistance. Funding provided by the Refugee Act of 1980 is administered by the Office of Economic Assistance, Department of Social Services, Pierre. The bulk of the funds are dispensed on the basis of a contract with Lutheran Social Services for English Language and Referral Services for Refugees (Sioux Falls). The pay caseload has remained about forty, but the numbers of adults and children involved have dropped about 50% since 1981. Funding has decreased from a high of $257,770 in 1982 to an estimated $193,848 in 1984.

(6) General Revenue Sharing. Under the Fiscal Assistance to State and Local Government Act, enacted in 1972, South Dakota received $24,119,000 as its initial allocation. The state's share not now funded, was one-third with the remainder distributed to local general purpose governments. Following is the initial distribution as compared with recent allocations (000's omitted).

	County	City	Township	Tribal Gov'ts	Total
1972	9,530	4,781	1,203	565	16,079
1981	7,998	5,380	1,669	965	16,012
1982	7,260	5,827	1,182	379	14,650
1983	7,361	6,538	1,228	795	15,924
1984	6,844	6,444	1,160	711	15,160

The state has lost compared to other states because of relatively slow population growth and low tax effort. When allowance is made for the decreasing value of the dollar, the significance of this program has declined. Nevertheless, since 1972 South Dakota state and local governments have received more than $225 million dollars in revenue sharing funds. The impact on the local budgets is to be found in the flexibilty and wide variety of uses. First quarterly payments (FY '84) for Sioux Falls totalled $307,531; Rapid City, more than $180,000; Aberdeen $110,478; Pierre, $25,567; and Yankton $42,543.

Second Section: Special Developments and Analyses

E. The 1983 Initiatives

(1) The Job Training Partnership Block Grant. The overall impacts of the Reagan program were to be softened by two developments in 1983. On October 13, 1982, the president signed the Job Training Partnership Act of 1983 (JTPA), the purpose of which was to prepare youth and unskilled adults for entry into the labor force. This program, designed to afford job training to the economically disadvantaged and others facing serious barriers to employment, stressed on-the-job training, skill training, and industrial-based training, and contained a private sector emphasis. In February, 1983 the governor appointed the South Dakota Private Industry Council to be the administering entity and grant recipient. The entire state was designated as the single service delivery area. The PIC has planned to service approximately 800 JTPA-eligible individuals with on-the-job-training at an estimated cost of $900 per participant; this goal has been exceeded.

The magnitude of the changes in job training programs can be appreciated by examining the funding changes which have taken place. The federal funding for job training since 1981 has been as follows:

	Total	CETA	JTPA
1981	$14,568,509	$8,621,559	$ ....
1982	9,693,240	4,861,693	....
1983	9,944,789	5,209,196	206,697
1984 (est.)	10,954,872	....	6,674,481

(Note: entries do not include carry-overs -- $2,365,930 in 1981; $1,304,111 in 1982; and $1,124,932 in 1983.)

The 1981 allocation included $8,459,367 for CETA job training services, and this was cut to $4,099,594 with elimination of PSE.

How serious has been the loss of the CETA-PSE money? How have the training cuts affected potential recipients? How have governments and non-profit organizations been affected? Program indicators of the State Department of Labor show that 880 PSE clients were served in 1981, none in 1982. The number receiving training in 1981 was 6,517; it fell to 5,320 in 1982 but then picked up to 5,472 in 1983. The number of adult job training participants who entered employment has remained at approximately 57%, with youth placement at about

40%. In view of the state's low rate of unemployment, the lack of extensive training programs has not been regarded as a crisis situation.

The funds available under JTPA in FFY 1984 are over $4 million less than the total funds available to FFY 81 under the Comprehensive Employment and Training Act (CETA). This statment is somewhat misleading since CETA had the tendency to carry over funds from one year to another. The extent to which JTPA funds will carry over into FFY 85 is not now known.

There are less exact requirements under JTPA for target groups than under CETA. Under CETA, the target groups had to be served in the same proportion that the target groups were represented in the population. Youth, dropouts, and AFDC recipients are the major target groups of JTPA. There is less emphasis on public sector employment under JTPA than there was under CETA.

The brunt of the cuts are being borne by the public sector. Public sector on-the-job training must be in the same ratio as public sector jobs are to private sector jobs. CETA had a complex formula for the allocation of funds for target groups. In the first year, JTPA used that formula. Now JTPA uses census date for the proportion of funds for target groups. During the first six months of JTPA (October 1, 1983 to March 31, 1984), the 1,108 participants consisted of 598 males, 510 females; 218 drop-outs, 523 high school graduates, 288 post-high school graduates; and 991 whites, eight blacks, ten Hispanics, ninety-two native Americans, and seven Asians. Nine percent were on public assistance. JTPA funds are distributed directly to Indian tribes.

Since the emphasis in selection by both private industry and job service is on placement, some "creaming" takes place. To insure a high level of success in training and placement, those less motivated and more economically and educationally disadvantaged are least apt to be selected as participants. The shortage of funds for training stipends aggravates this situation.

A major impact of the shift from CETA to JTPA has been in administration. Under CETA, Minnehaha County as a metropolitan area was a prime sponsor with the "balance of state" being the other prime sponsor. The JTPA population requirement of 200,000 eliminated Minnehaha County as an automatic sponsor and sufficient area additions could not be made. As a consequence, in 1984 the Minnehaha office closed and all JTPA activities now are administered by the state. To simplify administration, fourteen members of the State Job Training Coordinating Council (nineteen members) are also members of the Private Industry Council (PIC, sixteen members). The PIC, which meets regularly, has stated its intention of placing special emphasis on economic development. State government has retained a higher percentage of grant funds than previously. Most of the JTPA training is done as on-the-job training by the private sector or by local education agencies or area vocational-technical schools. Since JTPA allotments are lower than CETA allotments, the amount of administrative money is less and staff has been reduced.

(2) The Emergency Jobs Bill. The second 1983 initiative which alleviated some of the consequences of the OBRA cuts was the Emergency Jobs Bill signed by the president on March 24, 1983. Total dollars received was upwards of $15,000,000 and was distributed among some thirty-five programs. This amazing, one-shot funding injection made considerable difference at a critical time when carry-over funds were becoming exhausted.

Funding by the Emergency Jobs Bill came after the 1983 legislative session and therefore had no impact on budgetary matters as considered in the regular session of that year. All discretionary issues were thus decided by the governor, who designated the Bureau of Intergovernmental Relations as the implementing agency. By July 7, 1983, this bureau was able to report that all funds were in the process of being utilized and in a large number of cases, all of the allocations had been obligated.

The July 7, 1983, report listed thirty-five different programs as beneficiaries of the Emergency Jobs Bill. They were as follows:

1.	Community Development Block Grant	$1,104,000
2.	Indian Health Facilities	500,000
3.	Rural Water and Waste Disposal Loans	1,332,000
	Rural Water and Waste Disposal Grants	533,000
4.	Bureau of Reclamation	2,000,000
5.	Corps of Engineers	7,400,000
6.	SBA Natural Resources - Tree Planting	79,000
7.	National Park System fences	274,000
8.	Land and Water Conservation	359,000
9.	National Forest System	555,000
10.	Fish and Wildlife Service	700,000
11.	EDA Grant awards from Washington	N.A.
12.	Business Loan and Investment	N.A.
13.	Highway Funds	1,745,000
14.	Mass Transit (Sioux Falls, Rapid City, State)	179,000
15.	Aviation Infrastructure	265,000
16.	Low Income Weatherization	1,009,292

17.	Green Thumb	168,663
	Green Thumb U.S. Forestry	45,999
18.	Social Services Block Grant	483,132
19.	Job Corps	N.A.
20.	Summer Youth (CETA)	165,403
21.	Displaced Workers	77,782
22.	Maternal and CH Block Grant	470,400
23.	Alcohol, Drug Abuse and Mental Health	67,194
	Mental Health	134,127
24.	WIC	275,716
25.	Community Services BG	47,515
26.	Perishable Goods (Commodities)	N.A.
27.	Food Pantries	161,540
28.	Child and Adult Nutrition	140,360
29.	Handicapped-Architectural Barriers	115,000
30.	Library Construction	190,267
31.	School and Hospitals	320,000
32.	Agricultural Research	23,500
33.	College Work Study	N.A.
34.	Cultural Preservation (50/50)	1,440,665
35.	Veterans Facilities	519,000

It will be noted that major block grants were included as beneficiaries of the federal jobs bill. The governor had discretion especially with respect to these programs. For the most part the additions were merely incorporated into existing programs. The federal agencies (for programs listed above as 2, 3, 4, 5, 7, 9, 10, 11, 12, 15, 17, 19, 32, 33, 34, and 35) controlled many of the allocations within the state.

With respect to the block grant programs, fifteen projects were approved for CDBG funding. The Department of Transportation was able to increase its obligation limit from $76 million to $78 million. The additional $1,009,292 for low income weatherization was integrated into the existing program. The $483,132 received by social services was used basically to catch up with previous shortfalls. The $470,400 received for the maternal and child health block grant was divided up to meet needs of seven existing programs, including a $212,530 matching grant program. The alcohol, drug abuse, and mental health block grant addition resulted in $67,194 allocated to a DWI program and $134,127 for mental health. The community services block grant (CSBG), a controversial program as previously noted, received $47,515 and thus was one of the very few undecided expenditures as of the time the summary report was issued in July, 1983. The areas not receiving aid were education and various health programs.

While the funds provided by the federal jobs bill were expended rapidly and met specific needs, no great sense of urgency prevailed among administrators. Certainly, the ease with which they were incorporated into existing programs meant there were minimal administrative problems. With unemployment at such a low rate, there was no great demand for emergency job creation. Above all, the new funds were regarded as "one-shot" affairs and should not be included as part of normal operating costs.

F. South Dakota in the Courts

An important aspect of South Dakota's administration of federal funding programs has been the extensive amount of litigation. The three programs affected were AFDC, LIEAP, and CSBG. In all three cases the state sought to exercise what was seen as its discretionary right. In two cases the state sought to limit entitlements and in the other to deny funds to a community action agency. Thus, South Dakota was, in each case, seeking restrictions on spending. The litigation is significant further in that no attempt was made to seek a legislative solution. The courts were being used as umpire.

(1) Community Services Block Grant. Prior to fiscal year 1982 (July 1, 1981), South Dakota had the distinction of having the only state community action agency in the nation. In all other states, the local community action agencies dealt directly with the federal government. The state community action agency acted as a "pass-through" agency for federal funds to six local projects.

Under the CSBG as established by OBRA, the states received additional authority to effectively manage the funds provided under the program. South Dakota elected to administer the CSBG during the transition year. In response to drastic reductions in the level of funding received under the CSBG as compared to prior years, the adopted state plan included funding for only three out of the six local community service agencies funded under the former program. One of the three agencies whose funding was eliminated filed a complaint in United States District Court. The complaint sought to enjoin the state from implementing the plan. The basis of the complaint was a claim that the state did not comply with federal mandates in submitting the plan.

The United States District Court upheld the validity of the plan, holding that the provisions requiring public hearings and compliance with a specific timetable for submitting plans did not apply (*Southeastern Human Development Corp., v. Schweiker,* 531 F. Supp. 440 (D.S.D. 1982)). The Eighth Circuit Court of Appeals reversed the district court's decision and declared the plan as submitted invalid (*Southeastern Human Development Corp., v. Schweiker,* 687 F.2d 1150 (8th Cir. 1982)). The effect of this decision was to require the distribution of the CSBG funds pursuant to the repealed EOA provisions. The Secretary of the Department of Health and Human Services (DHHS) awarded grants as directed by the court to the affected agencies pursuant to the former EOA provisions. The governor of South Dakota vetoed the grants under the authority given to the governor under the EOA provisions. The plaintiff then challenged the authority of the governor to veto the grants. The district court held that the governor did not have authority to veto the grants because the grants in question were made under the auspices of the CSBG and not the EOA (*Southeastern Human Development Corp. v. Heckler,* 560 F. Supp. 925 (D.S.D. 1983)). This decision was appealed to the Eighth Circuit Court of Appeals and reversed, thus upholding the governor (*Southeastern Human Development Corp. v. Heckler,* No. 83-1585, slip op, 8th Court of Appeals, April 10, 1984).

(2) Low Income Energy Assistance Program. The second source of litigation was a rule promulgated in administering LIEAP. To receive LIEAP funds, states were required to devise plans to distribute the funds to their citizens. South Dakota's plan, which was submitted in 1982-83, categorically excluded from participation in the LIEAP all persons who resided in subsidized or public housing. Persons excluded from participation because they received home energy assistance through the Section 8 housing program filed a class action suit claiming that the exclusion violated the distribution priorities mandated by the authorizing federal legislation. The United States District Court, in *Crawford v. Janklow,* 557 F. Supp. 1146 (D.S.D. 1983), held in favor of the plaintiff.

The state modified its plan to provide that those receiving a heating allowance under the Section 8 housing program would have the amount of their LIEAP payments adjusted downward. This plan was also held to be in violation of the federal statutes and the court ordered the state to make full payments to the Section 8 housing residents (*Clifford v. Janklow,* No. 83-3092, slip op. (D.S.D. January 16.. 1984)). The decision was affirmed by the Eighth Circuit Court of Appeals (733 F. 2d 534 (8th Cir., 1984)).

(3) Aid to Families with Dependent Children. The final area of litigation involved the determination of eligibility for assistance payments

under the Aid to Families with Dependent Children Program. South Dakota, pursuant to authority apparently conferred by the OBRA, promulgated emergency rules to provide that ownership by Indians of trust lands would be considered an "available" resource for purposes of determining eligibility for AFDC. The effect of these rules changes meant termination from the AFDC program and the Title XIX (Medicaid) program if the value of the trust interests combined with the value of other real or personal property exceeded $1,000. The final result would be to diminish rather substantially the size of the caseloads and outlays in these two programs.

A class action suit was filed in state court challenging the validity of the emergency rules (*Has No Horse v. Ellenbecker*, Circuit Court for the Sixth Judicial Circuit, Hughes Co., S.D., November 23, 1982). This challenge was premised upon alleged noncompliance with the state Administrative Procedures Act (APA) (S.D.C.L. 1-26). Before a decision was made, the state decided to allow the rules to lapse. This decision was prompted by pending congressional action on legislation which would bar states from considering trust land ownership in determining eligibility under federal programs. This legislation was ultimately enacted and codified as 25 U.S.C. 1408, thus making the suit frivolous.

(4) Litigation versus Legislation. These three cases are significant in several important respects. The forum of choice for all aggrieved parties was the court system. None of the parties sought relief from the South Dakota legislature. In fact, the South Dakota legislature had little, if any, formal involvement with any of the decisions that precipitated these extended lawsuits. Another observation that might be made based upon the preliminary results in the above litigation is that the OBRA did not confer unlimited discretion upon the states to administer the block grants. In addition to the rights conferred on the states, the federal government seems also to have shifted some of the duties associated with those rights. These duties relate to obligation to defend rules when judicially challenged. The state no longer can say that is a decision made in Washington, but must vindicate policy choices made by itself.

G. Institutional and Political Changes

To attribute major institutional and political changes in South Dakota government primarily to recent federal funding trends would be an exaggeration. But they have had significant impacts in two important respects. Those federal trends have abetted the growth of state executive power on the institutional side, and on the political side, have emphasized the prevailing South Dakota conventional wisdom that government should be limited, economical, and conservative.

The federal programs which have especially augmented executive power and resulted in an increase in the importance of the state agencies are those which have substantial discretionary funds. It is these same programs which are most significant politically. They include the community development block grant, community services block grant, and wastewater treatment (where there are distinctly local implications for funding).

In 1983, for example, 180 grant requests were received for CDBG money, and seventy-three were approved. One of the principles used in awarding grants was to try to give as many as possible and to favor those with substantial "match." In the case of the community services block grant, only three of the six community action agencies were funded in 1983. In the wastewater treatment program, some $120,000,000 of requests are yet unfunded. Eighty-five active grants were supported in 1983 from the Land and Water Conservation Fund apportionment, totaling $1,323,697. In many of the other programs the governor has considerable discretion as to the apportionment among competing projects. Here the issue is not between localities but special interest groups -- for example, day-care as opposed to mental health centers.

An important political aspect of federal funding trends has been the general public's perception of the trends. The headlines in 1981 announcing pending "massive" cuts put fear in legislators as well as recipients. As the state budget officer observed (February 28, 1984), "The first principle is to scare the legislature. Then they will take the budget seriously. This year, the impression that there were massive cuts and the farmers' economic plight, made this easy to do." For the past three sessions, the South Dakota legislators have tended to be dominated by the doomsday scenario.

Two important state administrative changes took place in 1983, directly reflecting the importance of the new federal funding trends. The Office of Assistance Payments (AFDC), the Office of Food Stamps, and the Low Income Energy Assistance Program were consolidated in the Office of Economic Assistance in the Department of Social Services. This consolidation reflects, at the state office level, what has been implemented by a generalist case worker approach in the field offices. In the Department of Health, the Alcohol Community Assistance Program and the Drug Community Assistance Program have been combined into what is now entitled the Community Assistance Program, which contains all activities pertaining to grants to the alcohol and drug abuse facilities. These changes should make possible better coordination of block grant expeditures.

H. Efficiency and Management

One of the significant effects of the Reagan cutbacks has been the extent to which the changing financial picture has force the bureaucracy to reexamine its operations and reevaluate its priorities. In addition, it has placed a premium on innovation, and sometimes, to the surprise of administrators, new and less expensive ways of providing services have actually been more effective. Thus the closing of offices and the institution of a contract system for furnishing legal aid by East River Legal Services appears to have made possible local services not previously available. (See III-D-4.) Other good examples are the use of generalist field case workers made possible by the consolidation of the Office of Assistance Payments (AFDC), the Office of Food Stamps, and the Low Income Energy Assistance Program (LIEAP) into the Office of Economic Assistance in the Department of Social Services. Still another consolidation improving administrative efficiency was the inclusion of the Alcohol Community Assistance Program into the Community Assistance Program in the Department of Health.

A good example of the planning necessitated by the cuts that resulted in staff innovations is to be found in the "Plan for the Maintenance of Essential Social Services in Light of Reduced Federal Funding." This strategy plan developed by the Department of Social Services, January 22, 1982, was subsequently implemented as an "under-the-gun" responsive and responsible reaction to an urgent need to meet the changing fiscal picture.

Thus there has been created in state government a new emphasis on management. This was encouraged by a governor who was desirous of cutting costs in a responsible way. Furthermore, he was assisted by an able and mostly young staff in the budget and planning (intergovernmental relations) offices, as well as in the line departments. Nowhere was there substantial resistance politically or from the bureaucracy.

Good examples of the reporting on block grants are the "Legislative Block Grant Hearings, Block Grant Reports" (January 4, 1984) submitted to the Joint Committee on Appropriations. These are comprehensive, consolidated reports. In addition, the South Dakota State Planning Bureau submitted a grant proposal to the Department of Health and Human Services for $56,100 federal funding to enable the bureau to "evaluate last year's block grant reports presenting all the information necessary for resource allocation and block grant management and formulate an effective public hearing process." The grant was approved, and the project has been completed. The results have been published as **Block Grants: The South Dakota Story** (Bureau of Intergovernmental Relations, N.D.) Data already collected have been useful in the preparation of this report.

The Health and Human Services research project epitomized the new emphasis on management. The application noted:

"The primary research question South Dakota seeks to answer is: Can we improve last year's human services activities by using a more systematic approach to block grants? The activities previously outlined are desperately needed to demonstrate the benefits of systematic, rational approach to block grant management. After last year, no one can deny there is a need."

Finally, a comment should be made on administrative staff reductions. There have been lay-offs in the major departments, including education and cultural affairs, social services, and transportation. In a state where centralization is occurring (see III-J), there appears to be an almost dangerous thinning of supervisory staff, but this is a development that can be evaluated better only with the accumulation of experience under cutback conditions.

I. Strategy and Mix

South Dakota's state government is highly integrated. While the constitution requires the election of an attorney-general, secretary of state, state auditor, state treasurer, and commissioner of school and public lands, these officials are of lessening importance in the delivery of public services. Indeed, when a vacancy occurred in the Office of Commissioner of School and Public Lands, the governor combined the office with that of state treasurer -- an action later reversed, however, by the narrow rejection of a constitutional amendment in the general election of November 6, 1984. In another unusual move, the governor appointed the same person to head both the Department of Labor and the Department of Education and Cultural Affairs. The principal departments now number fourteen and are headed by secretaries who are appointed by the governor with the consent of the senate, but are directly responsible to the governor.

As a consequence of the well integrated governmental structure, a comprehensive, coordinated, and consistent approach to administrative policy is not only possible but does prevail. The approach to federal cuts and to readjustment has thus been uniform and purposive. The strategic elements have been:

1) to support as nearly as possible the administrative goals of (a)

economic growth with emphasis on attracting industry and accelerating water resource development, (b) insuring fiscal responsibility by balancing the budget but with no new taxes and especially no income tax, (c) maintaining essential services, including medical and social welfare services at existing levels, and (d) where necessary shifting resources to make certain that service levels do not decline.

2) to scrutinize administrative organization and operations with the objective of limiting bureaucratic growth. The governor has been especially critical of administration of higher education and the Department of Transportation. He has brought about a reduction in staffing in the latter from 1,478 in 1981 to 1,384 in 1983, and has plans to reduce the staff by over 100 by 1985. The district office system has been reorganized and streamlined, an unpopular political move. The entire administration is FTE and organization-conscious.

3) to seek innovative solutions. The governor, by example, has led the way: the purchase of the Milwaukee rail trackage, the sale of Missouri River water, the encouragement of out-of-state banks to enter the insurance business -- all proposals that required considerable "selling." This has carried over into internal budget adjustments as noted elsewhere in this report. The incremental approach is not sacrosanct in South Dakota.

The net result of these principles has been that most major proposals are the result of numerous lengthy meetings (many of which are interagency), with final decision by the governor. Department heads report that the top level considerations is never perfunctory, and often additional meetings are held to make certain no alternatives remain unexplored.

It should be emphasized that the present South Dakota governmental situation consists of a combination of relatively unusual elements: a strongly entrenched governor, a legislature overwhelmingly composed of members of the governor's political party, a relatively youthful administration due to a party turnover in 1978, and a legislature limited to an annual session of forty days alternating with a thirty-five day session.

J. Intergovernmental Relations and State Centralization

One of the issues created by the Reagan approach to federalism is whether since 1980 there has been an increase in the scope of state as compared to local government. The research by G. Ross Stephens

(1974) used financial responsibility, service distribution, and personnel distribution as criteria for determining the extent of state centralization. Table E portrays changes in state centralization for South Dakota and the U.S. for the 1957-1982 period.

TABLE E
CHANGES IN STATE GOVENMENT CENTRALIZATION FOR SOUTH DAKOTA AND ALL STATES, 1957-82

Financial Responsibility:	South Dakota	Average State
1957	49.8	55.7
1969	56.0	60.9
1977	60.4	62.5
1982	60.6	62.8
Service Delivery:		
1957	49.0	44.0
1969	56.0	49.0
1977	58.0	52.0
1982	67.2	53.0
Personnel Distribution:		
1957	48.5	41.6
1969	47.5	44.8
1977	54.7	48.1
1982	54.4	53.8
Composite:		
1957	49.1	47.1
1969	53.2	51.5
1977	57.5	54.2
1982	60.7	56.5

Source: G. Ross Stephens, "State Centralization and the Erosion of Local Autonomy," *Journal of Politics* 36 (February, 1974): 52-66; and from data supplied to the author by G. Ross Stephen.

Stephens observed that small states tend to be more centralized and if governmental costs are a consideration, they should be. Up to a certain point -- a point not yet reached in South Dakota -- per capita costs decrease as service areas increase in population. The 1980 census revealed that of the sixty-four organized counties, twenty-four had a population of less than 5,000 and no county in the state employed a county manager, either professional or non-professional. It would seem that the pressure for improved services would have dictated an even greater trend toward centralization on the state level.

The significant centralization moves have come in two areas: (1) education, where state aid has dramatically increased and (2) finance, where the state has assumed the responsibility for providing funds in lieu of the personal property tax abolished by action in 1977. Neither move was a response to any federal action but rather represented attacks on two state problems -- low teacher's salaries in the former case and deficiencies in administration with respect to the personal property tax in the latter.

While further research is needed, a preliminary survey of fiscal data indicates that the state is becoming relatively more important than local government in traditionally local turf areas: highways, law enforcement, welfare, and education. The increased role of state government is especially obvious in the field of education. The Department of Education and Cultural Affairs issues annual statistics on the "Actual Percent of Revenue for Public Elementary and Secondary Schools by Level of Government." The most recent data are:

Year	Local	State	Federal
1982-83	58.67	26.47	10.42
1981-82	61.12	28.21	9.43
1980-81	60.60	28.10	10.14
1979-80	65.32	23.82	10.86
1978-79	70.65	18.68	10.67
1971-72	73.59	13.85	12.56

What has been the impact of federal aid on the centralizing process? Has there been a change since 1981? At this point there is danger of giving the empirical data more weight than they deserve. While a rather convincing case can be made that state government is relatively more important in fiscal matters and as a policy maker, there is evidence that the trend, at least in South Dakota, had begun much sooner but especially since 1972, when executive reorganization occurred. The growth of federal aid as administered during the seventies did augment state power and made possible the development of the six sub-state regional planning agencies created by executive order in 1970. These agencies have been among the principal losers in the decrease of federal funds, as will be discussed later. Whereas they were regarded as potential representatives of and responsible to local governments, their decline further abets state control.

K. The Changing Roles of Local Governments, Planning Districts, and Volunteerism

Local governments continue to experience rather substantial increases in expenditures, especially in the traditional areas of police protection, highways and streets, utilities, parks and recreation, and health and welfare. The significant aspect, however, is that their role relative to state government's growth has been less spectacular; federal funding under the block grants has tended to favor state rather than local control in South Dakota.

The funding received by South Dakota local governments from general revenue sharing has dropped from $16,012,869 in 1981 to $15,160,857 in 1984, reflecting population changes. The most serious loss of federal funding has been in the wastewater treatment programs and housing. Highway aid, mass transit, and airport aid have generally been maintained at satisfactory levels.

Since 1970, South Dakota has been blanketed with wall-to-wall planning districts which have existed primarily from federal funding and which have more recently had to rely on contributions from local governments. The six agencies have experienced budget reversals as less money now filters down from the capitol. The loss in funding is shown rather dramatically in the changes from 1980 to 1983 in the budget for the South Eastern Council of Governments (Letter, D.B. Nielson, Director, April 6, 1984):

	Fed/State	Local	Other	Total
1980: July 1- June 30	$211,276	$134,257$	886	$346,276
1981: July 1- Dec. 31	251,397	143,478	3,457	398,332
1982: Jan. 1- Dec. 31	138,054	103,716	8,498	250,268
1983: Jan. 1- Dec. 31	114,213	83,518	13,638	211,369

The decrease in funding of the Black Hills Council of Local Governments (Rapid City) was even greater. In 1981 federal funding was 72% of its total budget of $607,000. This decreased to 22% of $263,000 in fiscal 1984. While local resources increased, the future of this planning district as well as the other five remains bleak (Ltr, Van A. Lindquist, Executive Director, April 17, 1984).

Another interesting development has been the rise in the use of volunteers with the elimination of PSE availability to non-profits. The Office of Volunteerism was established on August 1, 1982, in what is now the Bureau of Intergovernmental Relations. The office was initially funded by $47,300 from ACTION (1982), and this has been supplemented by an additional $75,000 from the community services block grant. The first annual conference of the South Dakota Association of Volunteer Leaders was held in September 1983 with over 100 in attendance. It is estimated that there now are 300 paid managers to volunteer groups in South Dakota. ACTION, whose funds have not increased, supports nine retired senior volunteer programs in the state, two foster grandparents organizations, Vista Volunteers, one senior companion program, as well as the Office of Volunteerism. The Director of the Office of Volunteerism thinks that there has been a slight increase, perhaps 4%, in volunteerism in the state since 1981, and points to the periodic distribution of surplus commodities at a cost of less than $50,000 with the use of 3,000 volunteers at a savings of over $220,000 annually as an example of volunteerism at its best.

IV. CONCLUSIONS AND OBSERVATIONS

A. What Really Happened? Testing Hypotheses

The reference in Shakespeare to "a tide in the affairs of men" has equal validity to governments. There are occasions when the speed of change in government accelerates and the position of a student of contemporary affairs becomes the more rewarding because the time frame is collapsed. But it is not always easy to determine what the ultimate direction of the tide may be. Perhaps there are undetected undertows. In this section what now appear to be the more significant trends are profiled and evaluated.

(1) "Economy and Efficiency." A main feature of the new federalism has been giving state governments more discretion to implement federally assisted programs. This discretion extends to both policymaking and administration. The primary federal objective seems to be to cut costs through reductions in funding. These reductions can be made up by the states utilizing their own revenues, by cutting the number of recipients, or by enhancing program efficiencies. It appears that South Dakota has adopted a mixed strategy, although increased efficiency appears to be the most acceptable approach of the three alternatives. An objective seems to be to cut costs either through improved efficiency or by simply providing less funds.

In light of the state's historical experience, it could have been predicted that the attitude of the South Dakota bureaucracy would be most sympathetic to the Reagan approach, and indeed it has been. Possibly this is the chief reason for the easy acceptance of cuts. The state's adherence to the work ethic made workfare an attractive program, and there has been great determination to make the program succeed. This philosophy is reiterated in the conclusions presented in *Block Grants? The South Dakota Story* (N.D.:80):

> The Bureau of Intergovernmental Relations has determined, after substantial research and numerous interviews with state agencies and provider groups, that although the funding cuts associated with the block grants do not further the cause of social welfare in

58

the state of South Dakota, the cuts did not substantially reduce services. The vast majority of respondents stated that the basic needs of the citizens were being met by some social welfare provider group.

Numerous programs do not require a definite showing of financial need to be able to derive services. While it may be beneficial in the long term to assist all individuals, the financial resources do not exist. In order to determine who should be the recipients of the limited funds available, the state of South Dakota would request that the federal government remove remaining restrictions in the block grant programs that require percentage allocations to various programs. Our proposal is to consolidate the following grants into one "true block grant": Low Income Energy Assistance Block Grant, Title XX Social Services Block Grant, Preventive Health and Health Services Block Grant, Maternal and Child Health Block Grant, Community Services Block Grant and Alcohol, Drug Abuse and Mental Health Block Grant.

In the area of the traditional "economy and efficiency" approach, a number of "pluses" can be enumerated:

1) the establishment of the generalist case worker position (forty-four at present) and the Office of Financial Assistance, which made possible a single point of contact for recipients of AFDC, food stamps, and energy payments;
2) the undergirding of the reorganized and centralized mental health administration, which embraces both state institutions and community mental health centers;
3) the improved efficiency and perhaps effectiveness in legal aid services by using the contract method;
4) the reorganization of transportation field offices;
5) the increase in private sector participation in job training programs;
6) the improvement of managerial capacity resulting from the necessity to innovate and provide "creative financing" and as a consequence of this, numerous, albeit minor, departmental reorganizations;
7) the substitution of state for national priorities (a plus if local determination is considered more responsive and responsible). Notable here have been the higher priority given to water projects in CDBG, the targeting of CSBG monies, and shifts in health funding;
8) a slowing in the rate of program cost increases.

What are minuses, as with the pluses, can be disputed. Here are some candidates:

1) less targeting to those most in need of assistance in the low income, disadvantaged, and minority groups. This is evident in JTPA, with its new emphasis on a high rate of placement and on job training rather than basic education, and in the distribution of CDBG funds:

2) a reduction in the number of recipients. The extent of true, unmet hurt is an important, unmeasured, and perhaps unmeasurable outcome. The low unemployment rate, while preferable to a higher rate, is not a reliable index of distress. Moreover, many unemployed have undoubtedly left the state.

3) no great dollar savings; in an absolute sense, few South Dakota programs are funded at lower levels now than in 1981. When allowance is made for inflation, the results would, of course, be different.

(2) Behavioral Responses and Hypotheses. How has the state reacted to the funding cuts? What accounts for differences by type of program and by agency?

1. The cuts in the entitlement programs have stuck and there has been no desire to have them changed. The public seemed to feel that programs were carelessly administered and eligibility needed tightening. In three cases the state sought even more limited eligibility and went to court to prove its case. (See III-F.)

2. Replacement has depended primarily upon the state's priorities. South Dakota has a very high proportion of the elderly (fifth among the states), and the plight of those in nursing homes is of paramount concern. Legislators are aware of the political potential of elderly voters. The Medicaid match is not debated despite the increases involved. Water development and transportation needs are being met. Energy conservation (weatherization) is augmented by funding transfers. Programs seen as primarily federal, such as food stamp or school lunch, do not receive the same attention.

3. Federal aid increases will be isolated from regular programs when they are to be perceived temporary in nature, as with the Emergency Jobs Bill. In this instance, recipient agencies are warned not to consider the additional funding as part of a permanent appropriation base. Where new money was received by agencies previously seriously cut, there was a tendency to regard the addition as predictive of future federal action.

4. The South Dakota executive branch dominated decision making with regard to new and old money, off or on the budget cycle, but it

is unclear how much of this domination is wedded to the dynamic character of the present governor and the common political complexion of the legislature and the governor. Thus, if the legislature (or even one house) were of the opposite political party, or the governor was less energetic and knowledgeable, the situation might very well be somewhat different.

5. South Dakota, as apparently typical of rural states, is becoming more and more centralized. The increased use of state authority of CDBG and CSBG as well as in education cannot but mean an aggrandizement of state vis-a-vis local government. Rural government tends to be "lobby-proof." The typical special interest advocate has neither the time nor resources to contact and influence sixty-six counties and over 300 municipalities when they are of such relative unimportance. Under these circumstances, the increase of state authority is inevitable and the new funding approach has abetted it.

6. The growing role of non-profits, especially in shelter and meal programs, has probably been inevitable in the light of social service cutbacks.

7. The process of centralization in South Dakota has proceeded rapidly in the past decade, much faster than in the sister states. In both North Dakota and Nebraska, greater welfare activities take place on the local level. When the mechanism for integration and centralization is in place -- as it has been in South Dakota since the adoption of a constitutional amendment in 1972 authorizing and requiring executive reorganization -- the pace of change will most probably increase as service demands grow and financial resources lag.

8. The hypothesis seems valid in South Dakota that where there is an integrated executive branch, creative financing and management are more readily achieved. The past three years have seen more changes in minor yet significant administrative organization and procedures than in all the past thirty years. Changes in federal funding have been an important and productive catalyst.

In retrospect, the federal funding changes and approach of the past three years were like "winds of change" to South Dakota state government. The three years have been a time of dynamic activity, and the block grant approach has afforded added opportunity to make changes in organization as well as in policy.

B. The Trend: Will It Bend?

There is an old limerick that goes like this:

A trend is a trend is a trend,
The question is: will it bend?
Or, will it stay in its course
Not yielding to force
And go to its inevitable end?

A trend at work in American government is the centralization of power in Washington. Long ago Beard, Corwin, Laski and others predicted the inevitable demise of the division of powers as established in 1787. The forces working toward that end seem inescapable and overwhelming, although ordinarily incremental.

The Reagan approach has been an attempt to reverse, or at least to "bend," the direction government had been taking. For South Dakota, as this study shows, it seems to be working at least for now. State priorities have been given an added boost. The state's administrative organization and managerial capacity have improved. Bureaucratic growth has been slowed. But only after a decade or two of political and economic changes can it be determined whether the developments of the early eighties were only temporary aberrations or constituted the beginning of a protracted and fundamental transformation.

REFERENCES

Articles and Books:

Advisory Commission on Intergovernmental Relations (1981) *Tax Capacity of the Fifty States.* Washington, D.C.: ACIR.

Bureau of Business Research (1983) "Trend of Business." *South Dakota Business Review.*

Bureau of Intergovernmental Relations (n.d.) *Block Grants: The South Dakota Story.* Pierre, S.D.: Bureau of Intergovernmental Relations.

Carlson, Loren (1980) "Dakota Proposition: Panacea or Nightmare for South Dakota?" *Public Affairs* 78:1-8.

Elwood, John M. (1982) *Reductions in U.S. Domestic Spending.* New Brunswick, N.J.: Transaction Books.

Merwin, John (1983) "Let's Make a Deal." *Forbes.* November, 21.

Nathan, Richard, F.C. Doolittle and Associates (1983) *The Consequences of Cuts: The Effects of the Reagan Domestic Program on State and Local Governments.* Princeton, N.J.: Princeton University Urban and Research Center.

Office of Education, U.S. (1983) *The Condition of Education.* Washington, D.C.: U.S. Office of Education.

Pierce, Neal R. and Jerry Hagstrom (1983) *The Book of America.* New York: W.W. Norton.

Satterlee, James (1983) *South Dakota Poverty Trends,* 1970-1980. Brookings, S.D.: South Dakota Census Data Center, South Dakota State University.

Sioux Falls Argus Leader (1981) "Cuts May Suck Millions From S.D." *Sioux Falls Argus Leader.* June 13, 1981.

Stephens, G. Ross (1974) "State Centralization and the Erosion of Local Autonomy." *Journal of Politics.* 36:44-76.

U.S. News and World Report (1984) "South Dakota's New Love Affair with Big Banks." *U.S. News and World Report.* January 30.

Letters:

Lindquist, Van A. (1984) Letter to Author. April, 17.

Court Cases:

Southeastern Human Development Corp. v. Schweiker, 531 F. Supp. 440.

Southeastern Human Development Corp. v. Schweiker, 687 F. 2d. 1150.

Southeastern Human Development Corp. v. Heckler, 560 F. Supp. 925.

Crawford v. Janklow, 557 F. Supp. 1146.

Clifford v. Janklow, 733 F. 2d. 534.

Has No Horse v. Ellenbecker, Sixth Judicial Circuit, Hughes County, S.D., November 23, 1982.

Program	FFY1981	FFY1982	FFY1983	State/Local Response
ENTITLEMENT GRANTS				
1.AFDC	11,866,284	11,735,356	13,450,477	See III-A-1.
2.Medicaid	51,822,340	52,215,645	55,922,542	1984 est. 67,653,000 See III-A-2.
3.Food Stamps	22,217,611	23,808,774	26,866,344	1984 est. 27,563,878 See III-A-3.
*4.Child Nutrition	11,740,767	9,215,082	11,200,179	No additional state money, but federal funding restored. See III-A-4.
5.Refugee Assistance	233,029	257,780	207,995	1984 est. 193,848 See III-D-5.
BLOCK GRANTS				
6.Alcohol, D.A. & M.H.	N.A.	2,511,000	3,140,000	See III-B-4 for breakdown.
*7.MCH	1,435,618	1,202,583	1,238,535	The state contributed $300,000 in 1981, $313,317 in 1982, and $350,000 in 1983. See III-B-2.
*8.Preventive Health	211,701	163,701	210,882	1984 est. $231,709 See III-B-1.
9.Primary H. Care	N.A. Projects funded from Regional Office			
10.E & S I Ed. II	9,079,814 2,000,000	8,855,210 2,000,000	8,960,516 2,187,360	See III-B-9. See III-B-9.

*11.CSBG	1,820,736	1,011,944	803,109	See III-B-7.
12.CDBG	6,111,000	7,057,000	7,856,000	See III-B-6.
*13.Social Services	9,176,163	7,270,604	8,013,225	See III-B-5.
14.LIEA	5,184,560	5,821,637	11,010,851	See III-B-8.
*15.CETA	8,621,559	4,861,693	5,209,196	Carry-over not included. 1981 -$2,365,930 1982 -$1,304,111 1983 -$1,124,932 See II-K-2.
16.JTPA			206,697	See II-K-2.
17.Voc Rehab	4,331,240	4,151,095	4,512,704	No change.

CAPITAL GRANTS

*18.Fed Highway	56,135,622	51,677,161	76,949,347	State matching was: 1981-$10,275,676 1982-$ 8,764,849 1983-$12,327,285 Jobs bill added $436,250 See III-C-1.
19.Mass	507,491	451,422	438,177	Matching by recipients was: 1981 - $131,947 1982 - $117,374 1983 - $113,926 See III-C-2.
*20.Airport Aid	2,311,952	1,824,259	1,972,021	In 1983 $128,333 was added from jobs bill. See III-C-3.
*21.Energy Cons.	3,202,681	1,932,495	2,490,034	1984 est. $4,056,496 See III-C-4.
*22.Wastewater Treatment	16,500,000	11,800,000	11,900,000	No state money involved.

				See III-C-5.
*23. Housing Sec. 8 (new)	278 units ($4800/ unit)			See III-C-6.
24. Housing Sec. 8 (existing)	38 units ($3700/ unit)	49 units	45 units	See III-C-6.
25. Housing Sec. 8 (mod. reh.)	88 units	26 units	3 units	See III-C-6.

OTHER PROGRAMS

26. Impact Aid	14,531,709	14,314,309	15,898,046	See III-B-9.
*27. Urban Indian Health	170,350	132,636	154,126	No state money involved. See III-D-1.
*28. EDA	N.A			See III-C-7.
29. Older Americans	1,300,000	1,300,000	1,300,000	State has added small amount to this popular program. See III-D-3
*30. Legal Services	See III-D-4 for breakdown			Some reorganization to effect economies. See III-D-4.
31. Arts Council	275,000	250,350	282,700	When this program was cut, legislature replaced. See III-D-2.
32. Com. on Humanities	324,000	324,000	324,000	See III-D-2.

NOTES TO APPENDIX

Data are taken from (A) *State of South Dakota Governor's Budget* for appropriate years; (B) data supplied by agencies; or (C) report prepared by Bureau of Intergovenmental Relations. Major funding changes are indicated by an asterisk (*).

6. The breakdown is as follows: alcohol and drug abuse, 1982, 930,325,; 1983, 826,725. Mental health, 1982, 1,580,675; 1983, 2,144,275. State appropriations for mental health increased 300,000 in 1982 and 1,200,000 in 1983. Tribal allocations are not included in the 1982 total. Exact data for 1981 are unavailable.

11. Carry-overs included in these data are: 1981, 605,876; 1982, 517,741, and 1983, 30,026. Only 229,277 was actually distributed in 1982, in part because of litigation.